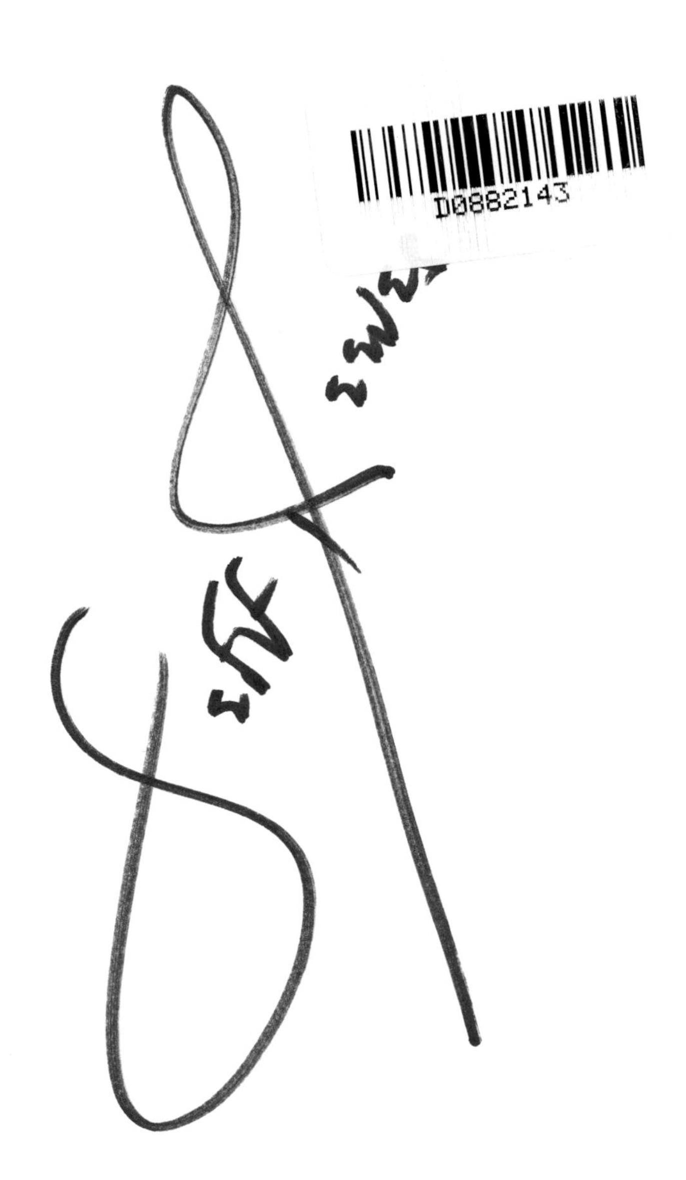
D0882143

The Art of Branding Yourself

Advancing Your Career Quickly

JEFF REEVES

with Freda Dents and Lindsay Williams

authorHOUSE®

AuthorHouse™
1663 Liberty Drive, Suite 200
Bloomington, IN 47403
www.authorhouse.com
Phone: 1-800-839-8640

First published by AuthorHouse 8/20/2008

ISBN: 978-1-4389-0121-3 (sc)

Library of Congress Control Number: 2008906138

Printed in the United States of America
Bloomington, Indiana

This book is printed on acid-free paper.

Mr. Reeves' sincerest quality has been his commitment and dedication to coaching and developing others. That has been the trademark indicator of the professionalism and business acumen with which he has carried himself through the course of our acquaintance. His leadership and mentorship have been very instrumental in catapulting my career to new heights.

-Je'Mone Smith, former AVP-Human Resources, Alliance Life Insurance

Jeff Reeves is first and foremost a master mentor who consults to corporate leaders and community service organizations. I value the advice and counsel he has provided to me throughout my career and the assistance he has offered in helping me develop and live my brand.

-Christine M. Glasco, Executive Coach, CG Consulting Group

Jeff Reeves is a man of vision and compassion for developing leaders...read, learn, and grow!

-Carter D Womack, President & CEO, Leadership At Its Best, LLC

Jeff Reeves has written a book that can help you set yourself apart from the rest. In this day and age where the race is long and hard, it important to take note that often your most supportive and vocal mentor is you! Jeff has taken control of his own success and offers sage and trustworthy advice on how you can reach your own self-actualization.

-Paula Allen-Meares, Dean, Norma Radin Collegiate Professor of Social Work, and Professor of Education, University of Michigan School of Social Work

It inspired me to build a strong professional network of experts and other resources. It also spurred me to learn how to ask the right questions to help identify the real problem, so I could harness the best resources for the solution. Now, in today's hyper-speed, mega-wired world, the standard for "plugging up your ignorance within twenty-four hours" has been cut to less than twelve hours!

-Lee J. Colan, Ph.D., Author of *7 Moments…that Define Excellent Leaders*

In today's global market, you are competing for jobs, opportunity, and your very future with people all over the world. Jeff's book is a perfect guide for how to do that, and you couldn't learn from a better teacher. He is one of the most powerful executives I have ever worked with, and when he is giving you advice on how to build your business, career, and personal brand—take it."

-Chris Majer, CEO, Human Potential Project

My advice to young people is, if you are the smartest one in your group, your group is too small. I have watched Jeff over the past few years as his son and my son have become best friends. He is consistent and caring when it comes to those he comes in contact with. I have sent some aspiring young businesspeople his way for advice, and he has accommodated them all. He knows how to help people brand themselves in a distinctive way. I have also watched him make time for his family and keep everything as much as possible in balance.

-Dr. Keith A. Troy, Pastor, New Salem Missionary Baptist Church

Jeff Reeves' book, *The Art of Branding Yourself,* will keep you moving forward to greater success when it comes to branding yourself. He has the inner edge on branding because of his years playing in the NFL and his years of experience in Human Resources. If you need help with making yourself brand-able, then this is the book for you."

-Wally Amos
www.unclewallys.com
www.chipandcookie.com
www.wallyamos.com
www.readitloudfoundation.org

In the area of personal branding, I have found Jeff's approach to be consistent and unflappable. He is conscious of his personal brand, it is in line with his personal ethics, and it is a hallmark of what Jeff brings to every encounter.

-Doug Reynolds, Former EVP and COO, Allianz Life Insurance Company

FOREWORD

Many people want to get ahead in life and in business. I have found in my years of studying successful people that the key qualities that one should possess include discipline. Discipline is a trait that Jeff Reeves has always possessed. We go back many years, to when I first became his business coach. He was at Sam's at the time, as the Vice President of People for Sam's Club, a Division of Wal-Mart, Inc.

I worked with and became close to him over the years and came to realize that he has a great amount of discipline that has served him well over the years. We have spoken about his time as an NFL player and the discipline it took for him to reach that status. Imagine that—one of only 1600 people in the world to play in the NFL! Now that's discipline. Jeff also has excelled over two decades in the corporate world. That requires great discipline too, and it's a large part of why Jeff Reeves always ends up at the top.

Another great trait I have found in successful people all over the globe is a trait of wanting others to win. Jeff embodies this caring trait. I have observed him as a father, as he coached and guided his son to succeed in his football career and in life in general. I have seen Jeff help others as well, mentoring them along the way.

As I travel the globe coaching some of the world's top C-level executives like Jeff, I now find myself shifting focus to the area of accelerating results and helping others succeed quickly. It's the focus of my new book, *Speed*, which is devoted to accelerating success using the foundational traits that the most successful people utilize (like discipline) and incorporating them into their business lives. I have seen the transformational effect of this philosophy, and I encourage you to sit back and enjoy Jeff's work here, within these pages, and apply it to your own life.

Tony Jeary

Coach to the World's top CEOs and author of more than thirty books including *Speed: How to Get Superior Results Fast*

INTRODUCTION

When you see certain logos, you automatically know which company is being represented. You don't have to guess when you see General Electric, Microsoft, JC Penney, Starbucks, Best Buy, Macy's, Nordstrom, or Nike. The same is true when you hear certain individuals' names: Tiger Woods, Michael Jordan, Tom Brady, Bill Gates, Lee Iacocca, T.D. Jakes, and Nelson Mandela. You recognize these names because they have branded themselves very well. You can do the same. Through strategically and wisely branding yourself, you can advance your career to the next level.

What is your brand? This is a question every company focuses on as part of branding a business, and one that most leaders consider. A brand is an imprint in the marketplace, and for a company, it's one of the most important assets. Your personal brand is much the same.

Every individual has a personal brand. It can be intentional or unintentional. If you are an entrepreneur or business owner, or a public speaker, your brand is critical to your success. It's how people perceive you and will determine if they buy your services or not. There is an art to branding yourself. Are you doing it right?

Surviving and thriving in the corporate world, as a minority, I have seen others make mistakes and have made mistakes of my own. Each mistake and new experience has been a lesson learned and has acted as a building block to my personal brand. My life is now centered on enriching others' lives, enabling them to guide their lives in pursuit of self-defined success.

You are a production of thoughts, a generation of conversation, a collaboration of stories and interests with an unspecified power to control your own destiny. Learning to control your own destiny with regard for different elements and tools that come into your life is necessary to foster growth. Growth defines who you are and what you stand for. When you embrace these things, it is undeniable that you have captured the art of personal branding.

I have come in contact with so many who do not know where to start their journey of personal success. As with most of the inquisitive people eager to start their trek to success, they would inquire as to how I reached the level I am at. The idea of creating an outlet to share my story with others was sparked with each inquiry until it grew into a blazing fire. Mr. Presentation, my speaking coach and friend, Tony Jeary, encouraged me to share my story with the masses and pursue my goal of enhancing the lives of those who are willing to undergo change in the effort to elevate their careers. With the support of Tony Jeary, inspiration from Bob Buford's book *Halftime,* and the pride and commitment of a North Dakota farmer who loves the Lord, family, and life itself ("the Commish," Richard Lawlar), I was motivated to share my success with others, like you, who have the same desires and drive that I began with and continue to maintain as I constantly expand upon my personal brand.

At a young age, I defined success for my life and set out to conquer each goal that has brought me to where I am. Throughout each page in this book, I will act as your personal storyteller, explaining my journey and hard lessons learned. My goal is to see you through this life-enriching expedition as you learn how to follow your dreams through self-inspiration, motivation, and awareness, as you grow and build your brand just as I have throughout my career.

Jeff Reeves

TABLE OF CONTENTS

CHAPTER 1

Mirror Reflections: Who Are You?

James 1:23-24… like a man who looks at his face in a mirror and, after looking at himself, goes away and immediately forgets what he looks like.

You wake up and brush your teeth—you look in the mirror; you fix your hair—you look in the mirror; you want to see if your new jeans look as good as they feel—you look in the mirror. The point is, there is not a day that goes by when you don't look in the mirror to examine your reflection. But how often do you really go deeper and reflect on what is deep within the mind of the very reflection that is you?

Through the years, I have found that people don't understand who they are. You may have this thought about yourself, but you have pushed it to the back of your mind just like the moldy leftovers in the back of your refrigerator. Asking people who they are generally produces a generic answer like "I'm a doctor," "I'm a teacher," "I'm a lawyer," "I'm an accountant," and the list goes on—you may have even filled in the question with your occupation. But your occupation does not define who you are; that is simply what you do. The real you consists of your life experiences—good, bad, or indifferent.

I was honored to speak at a men's retreat for a local church near my hometown. There were 700 men at this retreat, and I was there to teach them how to successfully prepare and execute the complete interview process. One of the most common mistakes of interviewees is that they are ignorant of the fact that the administrative assistant is far more important than the president of the company. How will you ever get an interview set up if you mistreat the administrative assistant who is in charge of scheduling the interview?

My goal at the retreat wasn't to give them a checklist to go through before each interview. Rather, my goal was to empower them through a branding matrix *(Exhibits 1A and 1B)*. The branding matrix was a tool to help the men see who they are and the reputation they have. Pepsi, Starbucks, Burger King, McDonald's, Nordstrom, Microsoft, and Best Buy are a few major corporations, but they all have a distinct brand in place to set them apart from their competition. The brand represents a certain quality and level of service that the customer expects. In the interview process, the person who interviews you is like the customer, and you are the corporation. Creating, establishing, and implementing certain traits in your behavior will brand who you are, thus allowing people to know what level of respect you command and deserve.

For example, everyone has an idea of how a minister is supposed to behave, but to see a man, who you know is a minister, cursing and telling crude jokes, you would do a double take. He would be damaging the overall brand of ministers. When you hear the names Martin Luther King, Jr., John F. Kennedy and Abraham Lincoln, what do you think? Respectful, passionate, driven, noble; these are men who built a positive brand around their name. However, there are negative brands as well that you think of when you hear certain names, such as David Koresh, Charles Manson, Richard Nixon, Enron, Denny's, or Hitler.

To give the men an idea of what building a personal brand is all about, I did something that is very rare for me, but was also necessary. I opened up to them.

My Brand

I'm a very result-driven individual who is very sensitive and giving. It has often been said that I care about others more than I care about myself. Personal brands are also built on your upbringing and past events that have molded you into who you are. Part of my brand was developed from having a tough relationship with my dad. He was very hard on me. We use to battle all the time, but I was my dad's favorite. My dad is seventy-eight, with many physical ailments today. He always worked extremely long hours every day and held down two jobs to provide for the family. He was perfectly fine during the week because he had to work but when the weekend rolled around, he would drink like a fish until Monday morning. When I became an adult, I asked him to go into rehab. The good thing that I can say is that I have always loved my dad. I have grown into who I am today because of the relationship I had with my father. He never missed a school event, game, or important activity throughout our school years.

By opening up to those men, they were more comfortable opening up to me. I discovered that every man in that room had something in his past that had changed his life and molded his personal brand. The problems ranged from drugs, alcohol, and homelessness to sexual abuse and alternative lifestyles, but that is not where the line for adverse lifestyles was drawn. They thought that I was there just to teach them how to interview for a job. Although that was the purpose for the talk, I knew there was a greater need than teaching them how to get a job. I wanted them to get to the heart of the matter—who they truly are. I wanted them to know that once they got in touch with their inner selves, they would be able to interview for a job with all the right tools. I wanted to convey to them that because they are different doesn't mean they are bad people; everybody has to deal with their own issues.

I wanted to give these men the tools that would prepare them to move to the next phase in their life—motivating them to get out of the rut and walk the walk according to who they were meant to be. Although my experiences were a lot different from some of theirs, we were able to relate because, just like you, we all had a past. Appreciating that the down periods in life are what lead us to where we are now is very important and something that you should constantly remind yourself of. I don't know what your current situation is, but simply because your life isn't perfect according to society's standards, it doesn't mean you have to stay that way. The truth is, I am no better than you, and you are no better than I am.

We are all in this together. The late Jimmy Valvano, former North Carolina State University coach, had the motto, "Never give up!" Think about where you have come from. What do you have to do in order to change? You must believe in yourself. If you don't, nobody else will. You need to look in the mirror and apologize to yourself. Say to yourself, "Whatever you are looking at, that belongs to you! Whatever you are seeking, it's seeking you—you can have it!" From that point, you must go forward and become the best person that you can be. Use your failures as stepping stones to become someone great.

Years after I spoke to the 700 men at the retreat, and they have had several retreats since then, the pastor says that those men still talk about the year I was there. It is not because I was a great speaker, but because I dug deep, made them focus on who they are, and touched their hearts by truly caring about their stories. I helped the men discover who they are, and in turn several have started new businesses and turned their lives upside-down in order to develop the brand they wanted to have for themselves.

As a defense mechanism, many people build barriers or mask their inner personalities to block others from getting to know what is on the inside. This is true for me as well. I have the chosen few that I allow to get to know me. This is because of the hurt that I have experienced in the past. I do admit that I have a guarded wall around my heart. There are some hurts that I never want to feel again. I believe that most of us are that way. We learn from our hurts, but many of them we never want to feel the sting of again.

Where do you want to be five years from now? How are you going to get there? It starts with branding yourself. Stop sleep-walking through life—live, and pursue your dreams. The only person that will limit your achievement will be you and you alone. You might be saying that one day you are going to have your own business. When you get up and look at yourself, your old friends in the mind meet you with statements such as "Yeah, but…." *Shoulda, woulda,* and *coulda* are staring you in the face. "But" is an argument for your limitations. Stop hiding behind fear and excuses to validate your actions. Build a case as to why you can do it. Constantly look for ways to live your dreams. Continue to develop yourself through reading and listening to tapes of those that have made it to where you want to be.

If you want to soar like eagles, leave the pigeons behind. Success is never-ending. It's always a bad idea to be arrogant. Make it your goal to imitate those that are doing things right. As you go along, develop a good reputation, because you will want to have positive answers to both of these questions: when you come into a room, what do people say about you? When you leave, what have you left? Your reputation is created by the standards by which you live.

Don't ever be afraid to ask for help, not because you are weak, but because you want to remain strong.

Another question to ask yourself is, how are others made better by what you do? I like to think of myself as being very consistent. I like to get things done. In the business world, I am very difficult to deal with because I'm all about results. I like to get things done—no excuses. People are constantly watching me, so I am very careful about what I do in public.

As you look at yourself in your mental mirror, you will find that winning is an attitude. If you can see the invisible, you can achieve the impossible. Your attitude determines your altitude, but not your aptitude. You have to recognize yourself—don't wait for someone else to define who you are.

Shaping

Think about where you want to be in the future, then write it out. The men in that retreat had to fill out a branding matrix. They were forced to think about themselves on a deeper level. Many of them were like me, very visual. I've been told that I am very intimidating because of my appearance. I have even been presumed to not be a friendly person. I look tough, but I'm just a big teddy bear. Because of things in my past, I have been shaped in such a manner that I let very few people into my world. I have been burned and hurt in personal business several times. I often share very little about myself. I am not a very trusting person. I must say that I respect people, but I am not trusting.

At the retreat, I told the men that as they look in the mirror, they could be happy or disappointed. If they didn't like the person they saw, they would have to do something about it. The same is true for you. If you don't like the person you see in the mirror, it's up to you to make the necessary changes.

I want you to believe that you can be the "Starbucks" of America. I want you to have a positive brand of yourself. You want people to see you and know what you stand for. I am a person of character, and I want people to know they are going to get a straight scoop. I take pride in being honest with people. I like helping people with the truth. There have been times in my life where I have been too honest, but nonetheless, I spoke what was on my mind.

I want you to step back and look at your life, where have you been, where are you going, and how you brand yourself in order to get better in church, in business, and in the corporate world. You need to understand who you are and how you are going to impart in other people's lives. Don't just think about yourself, but others as well. Your new mindset should be, how are you going to help others with the tools that you are using?

All of us know that the things from our past shape us into the individuals we are today. What has shaped you in a positive way in the past? What has shaped you in a negative way? Use the negative and the positive to move you forward into a wonderful future.

Many times in your life, you are dropped, crumpled, and ground into the dirt by the decisions you make and the circumstances that come your way. You feel as though you are worthless. But no matter what has happened or what will happen, you will never lose your value. Dirty or clean, crumpled or finely creased, you are still priceless to those who love you. The worth of your life comes not in what you do or who you know, but by who you are and whose you are.

Paying it Forward

In 1997, I started a foundation in Columbus, Ohio, for kids in the inner city. It is known as Athletes, Opportunities, and Kids (AOK) Enlightening Youth Foundation. Through this foundation,

I have helped numerous young people to attend college. The guidelines are that they have to maintain a 2.5 grade point average and they have to help someone else when they graduate. Those are the only two things that I ask them to do. A maximum of five scholarships are granted per year with the following criteria: two are awarded to state universities or schools, one to a trade school, one to a community college, and one to an historically black college (HBC). The AOK foundation also does after-school tutoring and preparation for the ACT and SAT. My goal is to help children through this foundation get off the streets. The whole idea of paying it forward is each one helps someone else.

Change Your Thinking

You can do more than you have done in the past. Challenge yourself to do more. Those who have courage, vision, and faith can achieve the impossible with power, feeling, and conviction to say, "It's possible." Tap into greatness, and go to levels you never thought you would achieve. This can be done through believing in yourself, believing in your dream, and motivating and inspiring others. Someone's opinion of you doesn't have to become a reality.

In order to be successful, you must be willing to do things today that others won't, in order to have the things others won't have. In life, you don't get what you want—you get what you earn. In order to do something you have never done, you will get to be someone you have never been. Retrain your thinking, and say goodbye to negativity. You can do extraordinary things by changing your thinking.

You are an amazing being. Humans are the only species that, by sheer belief, can achieve the most extraordinary things. Each of you is an ordinary person, yet you have within you the ability to do more than what you have done before. It merely takes an unshakable faith and commitment to your vision, to your dream. Dreams are hard work. To achieve them, you must believe in yourself and in your dream. You must be willing to accept that there are no guarantees, no short cuts, and no handouts. A dream becomes reality when you are humble, hungry, and willing to go the extra distance to accomplish your goals. You must also be willing to fail, but in the failure learn and use the knowledge to become stronger.

Negativity is a dream-stopper. It doesn't matter if you or someone else is being negative—get rid of it. It holds you back to the point of useless failure. Self-doubt, or the doubt of others, can eat at you until your dreams disappear. Having a positive attitude is everything. Fear, whether of the unknown or even the known, will stop you in your tracks. Overcoming fear makes you stronger. You can't be afraid to make mistakes, because if you are not making mistakes, you are not getting anywhere.

Never close a day or night without a positive thought. You never know when a loved one may not be there the next second, minute, or hour. They may go to sleep one night and never wake up. Don't go to sleep angry at a loved one without telling them you love them. The pain of taking folks for granted may have lasting implications for life. Stubbornness may cause these reflections of heart to engage in private pain.

You are special! If you do not pass on the reflection you see in the mirror about yourself, you may never know the lives you might touch, the hurting heart it speaks to, or the hope that it can bring. Count your blessings and not your problems.

CHAPTER 2

Value System Under a Watchful Eye: What Do You Stand For?

Consider this: the people who see you on a daily basis—what do they think about you? Your two closest friends—what do they say you stand for? Your enemies—what do they see as your inner foundation? Your core values and the basis to which you refer as the foundation in your decision-making process are ultimately what you stand for. Whether you recognize it or not, people observe and subconsciously make note of your everyday decisions, no matter how small or substantial. These decisions clue people in to your inner core, which is essentially what you stand for. Everyday life presents you with different situations, all of which have a variety of different stances to be taken into consideration and from which to choose. Whether it is gay marriage, the curriculum used by your child's school district, or even animal rights, the stance you take on any given topic is a reflection of what you stand for.

Knowing what you stand for is a reflection of who you are, and that's why it is so important for you to know who you are before you take a stand. This will hold you accountable for staying true to your core beliefs. You may be hesitant to take a stand because you fear what results could stem from it. Fear is simply False Evidence Appearing Real. There is a clear fear of failure deeply imbedded in many people. To avoid this, you must be confident in who you are and what has made you who you are—the events in your life, childhood through adulthood.

Forcing people to evaluate who they are is a way for me to ultimately discover what they stand for. When conducting an interview, I ask the potential employee a series of questions (*Exhibit 2A*). For your own benefit, I want you to answer the following questions in all honesty. You are only allowed to use one word, nothing hyphenated:

How would your boss describe you in one word?

How would your peers describe you in one word?

How would you describe yourself in one word?

I frequently ask myself the same questions to be sure I am who I want to be. My boss would either use the words *innovative* or *intense* because I take everything seriously and enjoy getting things done. Procrastination, and the practice of it, is something I despise. I feel that procrastinators are lazy and have not done enough preparation. Taking the initiative to immediately begin a task rather than putting it off will produce higher-quality work and hold a greater amount of professionalism. My team knows that if I ask for something to be completed by Friday, the last one to turn it in on Wednesday is actually late. My peers would describe me as focused, driven, engaged, and intense. *Passionate* is the one word I use to describe myself. I am passionate about giving, helping, and doing things for others. My passion is evident in everything I do and sometimes ends at an aggressive level of determination.

To excel in your professional career, you must also know where and what you stand for in your career. During evaluations with my employees, I ask them, "Why are you here? Why have you been here so long? What do you want to do in the next five years?

How are you going to improve upon your current processes?" Use these questions as a form of self-evaluation for yourself. As with my employees, it will assist you in understanding whether or not you are holding a position because you want to be in that position, or if you are there because it is what others want from you. You cannot do your best work or take the stand you want to in your personal and professional life unless you are in the position that fits you best.

For my employees who answer these questions, I help them to see the answers clearly. Then I help them implement a plan to accelerate in their current position or move them to a position which will help them to accelerate. I expect a lot from my employees. The amount of work I expect from someone depends on their skill versus their will. If you have skill versus will, I expect more out of you. If you have will but not the skill, then I can teach you. The burden of constantly having to motivate a person every day takes up too much energy and valuable resources. When a person wants to learn but doesn't have the skill, I am more willing to work with them. Those with skill but little will pull the whole team down, and I don't enjoy working with them. Which do you have, skill or will?

You have the ability to create a strong will and overcome anything in your present or past situation that hinders your success. My parents worked long hours, which left my siblings and me home alone most of the time. Trouble and mischief were a commonality around me while I was growing up. But, I had a strong will and sought out sports and church as my safe havens and outlets to keep me on the right path. From an early age, I knew that God had a plan for my life. I refused to accept or create excuses for possible life failures, but instead remedied the problem so that failure was not an option.

Trouble and mischief were not the only factors I had to avoid in life. Family members constantly reinforced negativity to me in respect to who I was and what I wasn't able to do. I was the only dark-skinned child in my family; my brothers were all light in color. I was told that I was average, that I had brown skin, that I was the black sheep of the family, and that I had stayed in the oven too long. My grandmother called me Smokey, and one of my brothers tried to tell me I was adopted. My skin color was not the only thing that set me apart from my brothers. With negative forces working against me, I turned them around and made them into a positive energy. I worked hard and was the strongest athlete out of all my brothers, but it also created jealousy from time to time.

Proof of becoming the strongest athlete in my family was evident in 1977. I was still in high school and was being recruited by most major colleges in the nation. The coach from Wisconsin, Cliff Knox, camped out on my doorstep every Monday morning to show how much he wanted me on his team. My father told me I was average and Wisconsin was the only school I would make it at, but University of Michigan is where I signed to play. The academics were more challenging, but that did not stop me from getting my undergraduate degree in three and a half years. At the end of my college career, I was signed in the NFL, but continued to study for my master's degree while I played and fought to be successful in my career.

Goals

Listen to your inner voice; always stay focused on your dream. The naysayers can be pastors, friends, or family, and they are usually jealous of you. Pursue and follow your dreams. Never give up! You determine your legacy and direction. Those around you can influence your legacy, but you have to make up your mind, and then others can support your dream. You can't make people do anything, no matter how much you encourage them. They have to follow their dream.

Following your dream requires you to dream and set goals for yourself. You should write them down, re-evaluate them every quarter, and modify them as you age. When I was in the eighth grade, Archie Griffin, a two-time Heisman trophy winner, came to my school. Griffin said three things people should focus on—*Desire, Determination,* and *Dedication.* You have to have the desire to be the best at whatever you do. Once you have the desire, you must have the determination to keep going no matter what, then the dedication to yourself that you can be anything you want to be. I started setting goals when I was twelve. My goals at age twelve were:

1. Be the best student I could be and graduate with a 3.0 average on a 3.0 scale.
2. Be a high school All-American in at least two sports.
3. Live my life as God would have me to and teach me how to be grounded and live like Him.
4. Be less temperamental.
5. Family—have God align us more as a family and see my dad recover from alcoholism.

I set these as long-term goals for myself, and they were based on my core principles and beliefs. I used them as a tool to reassure myself that my life was headed in the right direction and that I always stood for my beliefs. Goals should be reachable, but don't underestimate what you can accomplish. Mine were set at the highest level I thought I could reach, but I was wrong. I went a step further and exceeded some of them. Instead of maintaining a 3.0 GPA, I graduated valedictorian of my class. Rather than holding the All-American title in two sports, I received it in three—basketball, football, and baseball. There are also challenges in reaching goals. It took twenty-two years to achieve my fifth goal. Not until his fourth visit to rehab did my dad recover from alcoholism.

I have also set standards that hold me accountable for what I stand for:

1. Be a great dad.
2. Raise my children in church. Every day, I strive to be like Christ and become a better person. Studying the Bible daily is a constant I keep in my life.

Giving to Others

I am passionate about giving back to others. Driving through a neighborhood in Columbus, Ohio, one day, I noticed a school for unwed mothers. Visiting the school was not on my set agenda, but I felt led to stop there. The students at this school were poor, some were former prostitutes, and some had parents who were addicted to drugs. I talked to the director of the school for awhile and asked if I could talk to the young ladies.

The young ladies all had varied pasts that they expected would be with them forever. But I told them that their past did not have to align with their future. I told them not to use the baby as a crutch or an excuse to not succeed in life, but to succeed in life for that baby. I asked the women what they wanted to be when they grew up and how they planned to achieve it. To help them focus on the future, I wrote a check for $5,000 and gave it to the agency. The money was to be allocated when needed to help the women achieve the goals they set for themselves. My goal was to give back to them and, once again, stand up for overcoming their past and realigning their future.

Evaluate your life and discover what you stand for in every aspect of it—career, family, marriage, friendships, and personal life. Know what you stand for, make it clear to others, and help someone else find what they stand for while you exhibit a strong will to accomplish your goals.

CHAPTER 3

Stepping Out on Faith

Life is full of possibilities, but before you take hold of them, you must decide which possibilities will become realities in your life. Who you are and what you stand for reflect on you as a person and can either boost or devalue your personal brand. It is the decisions you make that exemplify your reflection to others. As a baby under the care of your parents, every tedious decision was made for you, but as you grew, you were entrusted with more responsibility, which led to more decisions for you to make. Each choice or decision in life holds a different level of worth toward your life and your future.

Growing up, I was a true prankster. None of my jokes ever got out of hand to the point of altering my future, but that is not to say it's impossible for that to happen. Abiding by the curfew my parents gave me while I was growing up was one of the first big responsibilities I had where there was a choice involved. There were two options: take heed of my parents' curfew or ignore it. My parents told me I had to be home by the time the sun went down or else I would have to pay the consequences. They would tell me that there was nothing worth getting into after the sun went down—only trouble stayed out that late. The decision for that was easy; I was always home by sundown!

Not all adolescents are wise enough to abide by curfew. You may know some, or you as an adult may look back, wondering what you were thinking as a teen with the decisions you made. It may seem like a minor issue, but for a group of sixteen-year-old boys in my hometown, this was not the case. I'm sure there were several small decisions leading up to the monumental decision that changed their lives forever, but choosing to stay out until one a.m. truly altered their future. They knew the other teens they were with were robbers and had committed a robbery recently. Even though they were not involved with the crime, they were caught with the guilty party in the early hours of the morning when they should have been home. Since they made the decision to associate with those young men, they are awaiting a ruling by the courts that could send them away for a long time.

Every decision you make will affect your future, even though the intensity of each impact will hit at different levels with each varied decision. The young men who stayed out past curfew lost sight of who they are and what they stand for. I know their families and the beliefs they have been raised with, and hanging out with the wrong crowd and ignoring curfew are not part of their upbringing. For whatever reason, though, they made the decision, and the lessons they learn from it are never-ending.

Decisions in the Next Phase of Life

Are you unhappy with co-workers or your boss? Do you want to be your own boss? Does the company you work for practice values that conflict with your own? With adolescence out of the way, you face career decisions. Making decisions about your career will take you places in many phases of life. The choices are endless; therefore making the decision is that much harder. To eliminate a few decisions for you, think about this: "Am I complaining about something I have the power to change?" If you are unable to suggest a way to change or solve the problem, then *stop* complaining. Life will never be perfect. Unless you can suggest a way to improve a situation and are willing to put a plan into action to solve the problem, then you have no right to complain.

Changing careers or pursuing more education is another decision you might be facing. I accepted a full scholarship for all four years of college to the University of Michigan. I finished my undergraduate degree in three and a half years. After I graduated, the Seattle Seahawks drafted me into the NFL. Easy decision, right? What college athlete wouldn't dream of being drafted by a pro sports team? It wasn't easy for me because it questioned who I was and the goals I had set for myself. I was raised to always look at the next step in life and see how that would affect my ability to achieve my next set of goals. I still had time left on my scholarship with Michigan, and I knew that a professional football career would not be my only career. When I signed with the Seahawks, I made the decision to continue working on my MSW/MBA while I played for them. Because I made education a priority, Seattle was willing to work it into my contract, and I was still able to finish using the rest of my scholarship at Michigan to earn my master's degree.

While other teammates were out living the life of a professional athlete and partying every free minute, I was studying and going to class. Staying true to my goals and not giving up on them has proven to be one of my greatest decisions.

Cracks in Your Foundation

Decisions concerning family and your community will arise throughout your life, and just like any other, there will be several choices, but you make the final decision. I have four cousins, two of whom died recently; all became comfortable with the jail system. Any time they would get in trouble, their parents would provide support. The concept of freedom was foreign to them.

Prison was comfortable to them. They made the conscious choice to commit criminal acts that led to prison. Although I love my family very much, when one of my four cousins called me and asked me to get him a job for the company I was working for, I had to refuse. He was asking me to falsify documents and lie to my company on his behalf so he could get a job. This always has and always will go against my morals and beliefs. Because I knew who I was and what I stand for, I was able to make a tough decision and not stray from my foundation.

Taking the leadership position in any situation has always been a part of my character. There was a high school football coach whose philosophy many parents and I did not agree with. He lacked creativity in his offensive scheme, and he lacked vision and discipline to develop the talent he had. The other parents pushed me to lead the rally and to stand up against him. Since I was passionate about the issue and did not like the coach's style or tactics, I led the way. We talked to the school board, the superintendent, the athletic director, and the head coach. But when it reached a public status, all the other parents backed down and left me out on my own when they realized he was not going to lose his job. It upset me, but because I was standing for what I believed in, I was still confident in my actions. However, I learned that although I stood up for what I believed, which was that the coach was not doing his job; I could have approached the situation in a different manner. I received a lot of negative press and was seen as the enemy. After some thought and reflection time after the situation had dissipated, I publicly apologized to the coach I attacked for my attitude and the way I acted towards him as a person. I told him in private that I did not believe he was a creative coach, but that as a person, I respected him.

In the situation with the coach, I made the right decision to stand against him because it was my personal belief, and I took a stance that was true to who I am. However, by placing him under public scrutiny and attacking him as a person, I strayed from my foundation of showing respect for others. I consider this to be a bad decision rather than a mistake. You may fear making a mistake, but it is only a mistake if you were not true to your core beliefs and if you were not able to learn from the mistake.

If you know you're at a point in your life where you know who you are and what you stand for, then you should listen to your gut when you make decisions. If it just doesn't feel right, then you're not making the right decision.

One of the biggest mistakes with my career was ignoring my gut. I made the decision to leave Pepsi Cola and go work for US West in 1996. With that position, I was following one of the smartest female executives I had ever worked with to the new company. Instead of listening to my gut, I listened to my head. In my head, all I could see was the surface-level glorification—money!

Catherine Hapka, the COO, was the individual who influenced my decision to join US West. But soon thereafter, she resigned some eight weeks into my start date. After her departure, I stayed another twelve months and became disenchanted with Denver and the organization. It was a very frustrating time in my career. I made some very poor decisions during the entire process and left the organization to return to Atlanta.

Making a major decision to change jobs or careers should prompt many questions. Asking questions about the company and the position you will fill is vital—do your homework *(Exhibit 2B and 2C)*.You can't trust your gut until you have factual meat to chew on before making a decision. Changing jobs should not be done in vain—for money, fame, or fortune. So long as your job is doing what makes you happy, then you will be happy. Status should not be your underlying reason for changing positions.

If you are impatient, your vision and goals will be skewed. When you're in the mood for tea or coffee, you should wait for it to brew slowly. The instant gratification of instant tea or coffee will never satisfy the craving of picky coffee- or tea-drinkers. In life, you should be the picky coffee- or tea-drinker and wait for results to occur slowly. Oftentimes, seeking out instant gratification in life will eventually set you back behind the line from which you originally started.

Late one night, I pulled into a gas station to fill up my car, and the only other person there was in a beat-up car. The man in the car recognized me. He and I had gone to high school together, and he asked me if what he had heard about me being a successful businessman was true. I told him it was, and then he continued to tell me how unhappy, depressed, and lonely he was, and that he wanted me to lend him two dollars to fill up his car, but gas was three dollars a gallon. I left, turned around in the middle of the street, went back, filled up his car, and gave him twenty dollars, since he had not eaten in three days. Helping him out was not an issue for those two temporary fixes, but I was not willing to put forth effort to help him in any long-term scenario. His hygiene was bad, the smell of alcohol was overwhelmingly present, and I could tell he was using drugs. These factors played into my decision to not help him long-term at that time. I gave him my card and told him that as soon as he was ready to help himself, I was willing to help him.

When you make a choice, although it may seem like a personal choice, it will affect others around you, not just you. One of my four cousins who loved to be in jail has made many bad decisions that will forever haunt their family. In an attempt to hide from the government, my cousin used his little girls' (three-year-old twin girls) social security numbers to get credit/state IDs. The sad thing is, he has ruined their credit, and they are only ten years old today, and when they turn eighteen, they will have to deal with the problem their father created for them. His choice was selfish, and because of it, they will suffer the consequences now that he is deceased at the young age of thirty-seven years old. They will have to deal with the setback he put in front of them.

Take action in your life, and make choices not only for yourself, but for those you care about. To accelerate your life and reach goals will help you do the same for those around you.

CHAPTER 4
The Invisible Chair

Abracadabra—Just like a magician who makes things disappear and reappear, you have the power to do the same thing in your life every day. Whether you realize it or not, everywhere you go, you are surrounded by people. There are two options: you can see them or ignore them. By seeing them, you can either benefit from them, or you can contribute to their lives. But by ignoring them, you are simultaneously slamming the door in your own face while slapping them in the face for underestimating who and what they are.

Seeking out solutions to your problems is key in life. You cannot remain stagnant and expect situations to solve themselves. Creating a solution-oriented mindset is vital. You must be prepared to give to someone else's life as well as be prepared for someone to contribute to yours.

At the beginning of my speaking engagements, I direct the audience to look to their left, make eye contact, and smile at the person. Then, I tell them to look to their right and do the same thing. By acknowledging the person on each side of them, they are taking the first step to expanding their network. To accelerate the networks in the audience, I have the members of the audience look at one another and say, "Whatever was impossible before you came in the room is now possible because you sat next to me." This is a phrase you should keep in mind at all times, and it is part of having a solution-oriented mindset. Until the audience members acknowledge one another, they are simply sitting next to invisible chairs; after the audience becomes visible to one another, they open the door to finding out more about the other person—the hurts, joys, passions, burdens, knowledge, and desires.

Just like you, I have sat next to many invisible chairs in my life and, of course didn't realize it at the time. Sometimes, it becomes evident to me many years later. There was a young lady in my junior high who was going bald; she was an easy target to tease, and like most of the students at the school, my arrow was pointed towards her. Looking at her appearance then, some would compare her to today's modern-day Ugly Betty. She wore braces, the awkward stage was in full force for her, and she lost so much hair, she had to wear wigs. One day, I went as far as to throw her wig down the hallway. Looking back, it was a terrible thing to do, but my immaturity and lack of respect did not stop her from achieving incredible goals. Today, she is a brilliant doctor with unmistakable beauty. Now that we are adults, she has forgiven me, but never passes up an opportunity to remind me what I could have had. Because I never took the time to get to know her, I closed the door to the possibility of having her as a part of my network of friends and colleagues today. The knowledge she had to offer is void to me because I allowed her to be an invisible chair.

How many times have you sat on an airplane, bus, or trolley with your headphones on or your phone attached to your ear and ignored the person sitting next to you because of the way they looked, dressed, or possibly even smelled? Not judging someone by their appearance is a tough concept to overcome. On a business trip to Oxford, Mississippi, my friend and former boss, Marvin, and I were carrying on back and forth, telling jokes and old stories. We weren't being loud enough to bother other passengers. So, when I heard a voice call out, "Hey, boy," I was a bit puzzled. I didn't know this man, nor did I understand why he might be calling to me. He was dressed like a hobo. His toes were hanging out of what were supposed to be closed-toed shoes, and he wore overalls and was a rough-looking character. I am African American, and Marvin is Caucasian. After I answered this unknown man who was calling me, he continued to talk about colored folk, make racial comments, and tell stories about African history. I was offended and told him I did not like his stories. As the passengers were exiting the plane, the man handed me his card and told me to call him sometime.

With the thought of invisible chairs in my mind, I kept his card, though his comments were highly offensive to me. When I returned home from my trip, I did some research on the man. I discovered that had I ignored him or thrown his card away, I would have never known that among many accolades, he was wealthy, the former president of a college, and very knowledgeable about history.

Not too long after I made his chair visible in my mind, I was scheduled to hold a conference on diversity. I asked the man to be my guest speaker at the event and talk on appearance. Onstage, he still portrayed the image of a poor man to the audience, but he captivated their attention and succeeded in educating them on diversity, views, and values. He helped me learn to appreciate and acknowledge the invisible chair, and I helped him, in a controlled environment, to change how he acted towards others who are different from him.

Traveling is one of the most common times for me to encounter the invisible chairs in my life, and I always try to acknowledge them. My son and I were walking through the Seattle airport when someone behind me started calling my name. We stopped, said hello, and chatted with the man for at least five or ten minutes. After we boarded the plane, my son started laughing, and said,

"Dad, you have no idea who that man is, do you?" I laughed back and nodded that I had no idea who the man was. But it was good for him to see that even though I didn't remember the man, I still took the time to acknowledge him. I took the time not only to teach my son a lesson, but also because I never know when that man could come back into my life.

Showing respect for people is another way to acknowledge the person sitting next to you. It doesn't have to be that you talk to them, but your actions are key as well. On another flight, I was sitting next to Whoopi Goldberg. It was a red-eye flight. All I wanted was to sleep. All she wanted to do was talk—the entire flight. I put her first, and instead of being rude, I talked to her instead of sleeping.

The invisible chair theory is closely related to burning bridges. More times than not, someone is watching your behavior and responses to every situation. Bad days are inevitable, but there is no excuse for treating someone in such a harsh manner that you forever shatter that relationship. Like most, I have learned some tough lessons in life and business. In my early years, there was nothing I would hold back—harsh words or actions were not unheard of in my past. I didn't learn to hold things back until the people I hurt would come back into my life unexpectedly. I have burned many bridges and then ended up having to work with the person later in life. It was uncomfortable and has taught me not to prejudge anyone.

Early in my son's life, at age nine, there was a child at one of my son's sporting events on his team who did not put forth much effort, and his lack of enthusiasm to be on the team really held the team back. Unfortunately, I didn't keep my negative thoughts to myself about this particular child on the team. I hollered and told the coach he needed to take the kid out of the game, and I even told the child he needed to go sit with his mama if he was not going to try harder, or he just needed to toughen up. Then his mama, who was sitting right in front of me, told me exactly what she thought about me. She was not happy with what I said—she was my invisible chair. I never took into consideration that his parents could have been sitting close to me. But, in the same respect, I think I was an invisible chair for that child, because after that day, his attitude improved, and by the end of the season, everyone noticed how much he had improved and how hard he worked. Although there was a positive outcome, I should have been more aware of my surroundings, which is another aspect of the invisible chair.

When I was living in Seattle, I also did a lot of business in Hot Springs, Arkansas. I was interested in buying a condo there so I would have a permanent place to stay when I was in town. There was a waterfront property I was interested in, and after setting up an appointment to view what I was told was an available property, my assistant and I drove out to see it. The realtor and a husband/wife couple greeted us as we got out of the car. The couple and realtor were taken aback to see a black man and a white woman together, and both refused to shake our hands. The realtor was polite, but after showing us the property, he said he had forgotten that it had just been rented two days prior. We left, and my assistant called back about the same property, and they told her it was still available to be rented. The realtor told me the same thing over the phone, but when he saw me, my appearance changed that. It was housing discrimination; they lied and put me in their invisible chair.

The invisible chair goes both ways—you can either be in it or sitting beside it. One you can choose; the other you cannot. Because it is your choice whether or not you're sitting next to an invisible chair, you should make it your goal to never sit next to an invisible chair. You have to put forth effort to make the chairs visible. If you are attending a large function or even a business meeting, you should always research and find out who is going to be there. If you are hosting a client meeting, you should try to have something they like there—their favorite flowers in the office, their favorite beverage available to offer them, or something else they are interested in that will grab their attention and create a common ground for conversation.

Wally Amos (founder of Famous Amos Cookies and now his new brand Chip and Cookie) is a friend of mine, and I am rather confident in saying that he has never sat next to an invisible chair unless the person sitting in it wanted to be invisible. As a conversation starter, he paints watermelons on his shoes and hat. He has encountered very few people who do not smile when they see his hat and shoes. This is his way of starting conversations with people he ordinarily would not talk to. His goal is to bring joy to everyone around him. In an Atlanta airport, he played his bazooka to cheer up disgruntled passengers in the airport who were waiting for their delayed flight.

Wally is a great example of getting people outside of their comfort zone. Even if you are not naturally outgoing, you can take small steps to pull yourself out of your comfort zone. Be a part of different groups that make you comfortable and cause you to interact with others. Take the skills you learn in those groups and apply them when you are away from the group, and the invisible chairs in your life will become visible. Be confident, and the people sitting in the invisible chairs can contribute greatly to your life; you may find a solid mentor or even a best friend—never pass up an opportunity.

CHAPTER 5

How to Become the Number One Pick

"Watching parties" are planned, where rowdy, die-hard fans sport their favorite teams' jerseys and the top five to ten picks are watched as they sit in conference rooms wearing their $5000 suits, only hoping for a five-million-dollar signing bonus. Every sports broadcaster has their opinion on who will be the number one pick, but when it all comes down to it, the teams have already decided who will be the number one pick. The day of the NFL draft is marked on fans' calendars, and since 1936, when it was put into place, on the day, the athletes have no choice but to anxiously await the results. On draft day, there is no more time for one last practice and no other opportunities to impress a certain coaching staff by scoring another game-winning touchdown. Their season prior to the draft is their interview. Every play they run, every pass they fumble, is noticed. They know critical eyes that could make or break their professional career are watching their skills.

Being the number one pick should be your fundamental goal in all aspects of your life. Just like pro athletes who strive to be the number one draft pick and who work out during the regular and off-season times, you must be working to better yourself and keep up with those in your profession as well.

As you search through an endless amount of job postings, you should notice that each one is very specific about the qualifications they are looking for their number one pick to possess. It sounds simple, but is oftentimes overlooked. Read through each bullet point under the qualifications section of the job posting and be honest with yourself. Do you possess those qualities? Are you able to obtain or work toward those qualities? There are several other people reading and applying for the same position you are. You have to have the desired qualities to end up as top choice.

The position you are applying for or job you are seeking will put you in various and different situations, and once again, you have to be honest with yourself. Are you prepared to handle the situation? Is your talent in those areas up to par? Observe peers or relatives who are in the position equivalent to what you want to do. Interview them and find out what tasks are presented to them on a daily, weekly, and monthly basis. Then put yourself in those situations. Are you capable of taking them on? Analyze the skill level the desired position requires and see where you stand on the scale. Standing at the top will put you as the number one pick.

Once you have undergone the simple self-analysis of your strengths in regards to the position, you must be prepared to go into the interview while playing your strengths at their highest level. Go into the interview confident. To overcome any fear you may have prior to the interview, go over it in front of a mirror. By watching and hearing yourself out loud, you will feel more confident when you walk into the interview. When you walk into the interview, look the other person in the eyes—this shows you respect them and that you deserve and command respect as well. Don't slouch—improper posture gives the interviewer the idea you are bored or not truly interested in talking to them. Your answers should always be positive and concise. If you are unclear on the question being asked, repeat the question to make sure you fully understand it before giving your answer. As you go through the interview, in each answer you give, you should emphasize your qualifications and what assets you bring to the table. By subtly adding in a few of your positive qualities to each answer, you will not overwhelm the interviewer with facts about yourself, nor will you come off as arrogant. If you do not have a skill or quality they ask about, you should mention the things you do outside of the job to better yourself and your ability to strategically handle meeting new challenges that could arise in the workplace.

After the interview is over and you have made a good impression, you want that impression to last in their mind until they make you the number one pick. Within twenty-four to forty-eight hours of the interview, you should send a letter to express your gratitude for their time and reassure them of how much you enjoyed talking with them. The letter of gratitude you send can also emphasize the qualifications that you have and how they fit into what they are looking for.

Strategy: Build it, Practice it, Implement it, and Be Their ***It*** Person

From the very beginning of your job search, you have to have a vision—what do you want to be, and where do you want it to take you? Aimlessly searching for a job will not get you where you want to be. Plan out your strategy and follow it through until the end, tweaking it along the way as needed. Your strategy should be such that once you have your first interview, they want you to return for a second interview. The experience of having you in their office for an interview must be a unique one and should set you apart from all other candidates.

Building a strategy to market yourself is vital, but perfecting the interview is the next step. Your resume is a key tool in selling your personal brand to the company you want to work for. A quality resume will help to ensure a first interview, but it is your performance in the interview that will determine where you will go from there. To be a unique candidate, follow the cliché saying,

"Dress for success." It works and will be noticed. Dressing in a professional manner shows that you respect yourself and the company that is interviewing you. Finding a mentor to help you practice the interview or perfect your interviewing techniques is another strategy you can implement that most of the rival candidates will not take part in.

SAMPLE OF A DYNAMIC RESUME

JEFFREY B. REEVES

8236 Kesegs Way, Blacklick, OH 43004
Mobile (614) 477-5008 • Office (614) 855-5129
jreeves436@aol.com

CHIEF ADMINISTRATIVE/EXECUTIVE HUMAN RESOURCES OFFICER

- Passionate, world-class human resources visionary and team leader with a P&L/operations mindset and success with four Fortune 100 companies in both union and non-union environments.
- Seasoned executive with key board experience. Oversaw Compensation and Human Resources Committees.
- Credited with having broad business knowledge and conceptual understanding of how functions integrate in support of overall business organization vision. Big-picture mentality.
- Builds world-class systems and organizations. Increases human resources effectiveness and credibility while driving costs out.
- Considered a true champion in development of people, programs, and policies through consistency and integrity.

DEMONSTRATED QUALITIES OF EXPERTISE

- Strategic Planning/Multi-year Staffing Projections
- Organizational Effectiveness, Growth, Restructuring
- Board Interface and Committee Accountability
- Mergers/Acquisitions/Expansions/Startup Ventures
- International HR and Operations Oversight
- Leadership Development & Succession Planning
- Performance-Based Management (Matrix-Driven)
- Change Management, Best Practices Benchmarking
- Shared Services Model/Collaboration/Partnering
- Executive Compensation and Benefits Transformation

KEY ACHIEVEMENTS

- Swiftly reversed six years of human resources atrophy by instilling a disciplined approach to business planning—quickly set vision, established mission for world-class organization, revealed gaps and strategic alignment to business, infrastructure, service delivery, and depth of human resources delivery for 100% compliance and execution (Allianz).

- Put teeth into performance management, achieving 100% participation by managers with more accurate assessment of performance. Drove succession planning, career development, and improved morale (Allianz).

- Improved efficiency, gained focus, and instilled accountability—implemented shared services model. Operationally ran five ancillary business units and consolidated support to service entire medical center, college of medicine, and office of health sciences, consisting of 15,000 employees. Reduced administrative costs by $4.5 million (OSU Med Center).

- Built best-in-class human resources organization that served as pilot for all new initiatives and benchmarked business practices. Designed several human resources programs (including pay systems, succession system, and exit interview processes) that were adopted by corporate HR and rolled out across all divisions of Wal-Mart Stores, Inc. (Sam's Club).

- Improved first-line management retention by 60%+, increased retention broadly in organization and among hi-pos, and enhanced bench strength—changed business paradigm among front-line management by building fast-track development and mentoring programs. Mentoring programs focusing on education and development (Sam's Club).

- Delivered millions of dollars in projected cost savings while successfully placing 93% of field directors into new roles—restructured and consolidated more than 20% of regional/divisional field operations, as well as flattened management layers by expanding span of control (Sam's Club).

- Directly responsible for transforming workplaces into diversified and level playing fields, i.e. transformed diversity status in only two years in revenue, market share, people initiatives, women/gender issues, retention, and safety (Pepsi).

PROFESSIONAL EXPERIENCE

2008- Independent Executive Human Resources Consultant and Author—Currently engaged in re-engineering and

Present reshaping customer service levels, accountability, and commitment to excellence for a US-wide HR outsourcing organization headquartered in Florida.

2006 - 2007 Allianz of America Corporation, Novato, California

A $20-billion North America subsidiary of German parent and the fifteenth-largest company in the world. Includes two companies (Allianz Life—life/annuity and FFIC—property and casualty) and 9,000 employees.

EVP/CHIEF HUMAN RESOURCES AND COMMUNICATIONS OFFICER 2007

SVP HUMAN RESOURCE AND COMMUNICATIONS OFFICER—Allianz Life Aug—Dec 2006

JEFFREY B. REEVES—Page 2

Key strategic leader in refocusing, recalibrating, and aligning HR as business partner within the enterprise. Span of control included HR, government relations, corporate communications, public relations, branding, charitable giving, and enterprise property/facilities, as well as meeting planning and events.

- Oversaw integration and joint consolidation of Fireman's Fund and Allianz Life HR function, taking out $15 million in cost.

- Consolidated compensation, payroll, and benefit systems.
- Recalibrated organization towards eliminating redundancy and reduced HR headcount by 60% while aligning efficiency and effectiveness.
- Provided strategic focus by creating Leadership Institute and Succession/Talent Management, assisting across Europe, North America, and Asia with the refocused commitment to strategic HR practices as an integrated business partner.
- Championed, with German parent, the vision and assessment for creating diversity training and building alliance teams worldwide.
- Systematically built an enhanced performance-based metric culture evolution. Reduced number of incomplete performance reviews from 500 in 2006 to 12 in 2007, as well as improved the rating distribution to more correctly mirror that of a bell shape and actual business results.
- Received approval to audit, re-create, and shape Shanghai HR organization.
- Built 2007 commercial and media blitz that successfully launched in May, 2007.
- Facilities team received team of the year award for bringing in new building project on time and on budget.

2003—2006 The Ohio State University and Medical Center, Columbus, Ohio

CONSULTANT 2005—2006

Leadership at its Best

CHIEF ORGANIZATIONAL EFFECTIVENESS & HUMAN RESOURCES OFFICER 2003—2004

Served as member of the Strategic Planning Executive Team and Medical Center Executive Committee.

- Instituted new Med Center Succession and Talent Management Process and Leadership Institute.
- Reshaped a metrics-driven, strategically-aligned HR organization; evaluated and began upgrading team of 150 HR professionals. Reduced HR headcount by 30% and drove out $4.5 million in HR costs.
- Implemented new IT Technology and Shared Services structure for entire Health System.
- Fostered accountability. Renewed focus on performance management with integrated leadership competencies.
- Led all change management initiatives through assessments, 360° surveys, retreats, mini-sessions, etc.

1999—2002 Sam's Club, Bentonville, Arkansas

A $43-billion division of Wal-Mart Stores, Inc., and the second largest warehouse club in the US, employing more than 100,000 employees in 650+ stores worldwide.

SENIOR VICE PRESIDENT & CHIEF HUMAN RESOURCE OFFICER

Recruited to transform an under-performing HR team of 7 direct reports and 56 associates into a strategically-focused business partner in driving aggressive growth and market expansion. Member of the Executive Leadership Team, reported directly to the CEO.

- Leveraged expertise in change management, management development, and benchmarking business practices to
- Completely overhaul HR infrastructure and key relationships.
- Launched Leadership Strategy Summit, identifying and accelerating high potentials throughout the enterprise.
- Developed and piloted New Field Pay System across three markets. Sold concept to Board of Directors.
- Innovative cost-neutral pay plan resulted in higher quality of hire, improved retention, and increased staffing flexibility. Pilot was expanded to 200 stores, and practices adopted by Wal-Mart, Inc.
- Championed corporate initiative that trained Wal-Mart HR executives in performance management and succession planning tools to promote excellence.
- Conceived and implemented Sam's Club University, training 2,800+ Field Managers.
- Engaged in assessment/feasibility studies for mergers/ acquisitions/expansions into Canada, Puerto Rico,

UK, and Japan, working very closely with Expatriate Program Administration.

1998—1999 Federated Systems Group, Atlanta,

Georgia IT Services Division of the $15.5-billion largest upscale department store retailer in the US, operating 460 stores in 34 states, Puerto Rico, and Guam under Macy's, Bloomingdale's and regional chain names); 1,300 employees.

CONSULTANT TO HUMAN RESOURCES ORGANIZATION

Supported the Chairman/CEO and President as a Consultant/ Advisor.

JEFFREY B. REEVES—Page 3

- Positioned organization as employer of choice through leveraging outreach, college relations, technical recruiter relationships, and employee referrals, enhancing market visibility and attracting high-caliber talent.
- Outlined three-year business plan with new recruitment/ training programs and changes to compensation, performance management, and career development.
- Accelerated recruitment and training process by 25%, capitalizing on technology to build a complete recruitment and training intranet; introduced alternative marketing strategies and field training modules.
- Shifted HR from an administrative function into a strategic business group actively involved in day-to-day business operations and a key advisor/supporter to leadership teams on strategy, diversity, and legal/ regulatory compliance.

1996—1997 US West Communications (Qwest), Denver, Colorado

A $13-billion "Baby Bell" telecommunications company with 18,000 employees in 14 states.

VICE PRESIDENT OF HUMAN RESOURCES

Served as Corporate Change Agent and Strategic HR/Operations Leader for startup of three new lines of business.

- Recognized as a strong, matrix-driven leader and key partner in executing a customer-focused and market-based business strategy to access business acquisition and merger potential for start-up businesses.
- Drove 50% staffing cycle-time reduction by streamlining process.
- Designed/launched mentorship program, new hire orientation/integration process, succession plans, and competency models transformation of multiple-site human resources organization from a non-strategic personnel function to a leaner, more professional, business-focused, performance–based, and diverse team in less than one year.

1994—1996 Pepsi-Cola Company, Inc., Atlanta, Georgia

A $650-million business unit of Pepsi, with 3,300 sales and operations personnel in 12 regional markets.

DIRECTOR OF HUMAN RESOURCES

- Transitioned HR organization from #12 to #2-ranked regional HR organization in the company in one year while cutting headcount by 30% and upgrading talent, realigning duplication, and broadening coverage area.

- Designed succession plan that increased focus on promoting from within. Drove a 2-point increase in employee morale and improved employee retention rate by 10%.
- Achieved a six-fold increase in female representation and reduced minority turnover by 7%.

1984—1994 Scott Paper/Weyerhauser Company, Pennsylvania, Alabama, New Jersey, and Washington

Multi-line union and non-union manufacturer with multiple plants and up to 4,500 employees per site.

DIRECTOR OF LABOR RELATIONS 1991—1994

Earned reputation for fairness, integrity, and mutual respect among seven unions and drove numerous process improvement and changed management initiatives.

HUMAN RESOURCE/OPERATIONAL EFFECTIVENESS MANAGER 1989—1991

SENIOR LABOR RELATIONS SPECIALIST 1988—1989

LABOR RELATIONS SPECIALIST 1986–1987

EMPLOYEE RELATIONS MANAGER 1985–1986

HUMAN RESOURCE / LABOR RELATIONS INTERN 1984–1985

EDUCATION

Master of Business Administration (MBA/MSW) in Social/Policy Administration

Bachelor of Science in Literature, Science, and Arts (Criminal Law), University of Michigan (U of M), Ann Arbor, Michigan

RECOGNITION

International Who's Who Professionals—three times/ Outstanding Young Men in America— five times

Human Visionary Award—Who's Who in Black Columbus

Recipient of Mobile Sports Hall of Fame Award

Society for Human Resource Management (SHRM)/National Black Human Resources Association (NBHRA)

PUBLICATIONS

Author: *The Art of Branding Yourself: Advancing Your Career Quickly,* pending release third quarter, 2008

Author: *Parental Guidance: From the Neighborhood to the Board Room,* to be released September, 2008

Author Insert: *For Buckeye Fans Only* by Rich Wolfe, Chapter 3, pages 112-118

PRESENTATIONS

Keynote Address -SHRM—Southeast Regional – 2002 (HR as a Business Partner)

Business School Morgan State University – 2001 (Theory of Change in Corporate America)

Florida A&M University Advisory Council – 2003 (Commitment to Excel)

"SIFE" West Coast Regional Conference - 2003 (Focus on Business Strategy – Leading Example

FRASERNET Conference, Cleveland, Ohio – 2002 (Mentoring and Developing Others)

A host of non-profit and church key note/ lecture series addresses on many topics

Additional Certificates and Coursework

The Certificate in Employee Relations Law, Institute for Applied Management (IAML)

Objectives, Principles, Terminology, and Regulations of Employee Compensation

EEO Employee Rights Seminar (Basic & Advanced Courses)

Negotiating and Administrating, School of Business Administration, University of Michigan

Managing for Inspired Performance and Relationships, Atlanta Consulting Group

Management of Quality & Productivity, Dr. Deming

Personal Mastery & Team Learning: Mastering Organizational Change, Personal Empowerment

Consulting 101: Managing & Leading Change

People Soft 7.0—HR Systems

Microsoft Solutions Framework

Phi Beta Sigma Fraternity—HR Committee Great Lakes Region

Board of Directors/Business Affiliations:

Arkansas Legislative Committee for Arkansas
Business Health Coalition Committee

North Carolina High School Dropout and Drug
Abuse Task Force, New Bern, North Carolina

Carver State Technical College Foundation, Mobile, Alabama

American Heart Association

American Red Cross

Senior Bowl, Mobile, Alabama

Sickle Cell Disease Association

Board Member of Cumberland County
United Way of South Jersey

Former Inroads Program Liaison

National Lead Program Former Corporate Liaison

Active Board Member, League of Black Women

FAMU Business School Advisory Board

International Mass Retail Association/Former Vice Chairman

Retail Hospitality Forum

Advisory Board for the Columbus Montessori School Campaign

University of Arizona Business School Advisory Board

National Kidney Foundation

Gahanna School Advisory Committee

Activities/Awards

University of Michigan, Assistant Academic Counselor, Ann Arbor, Michigan

Former Director of Bible Training Union, BTU

Former Director of Vacation Bible School, New Hope Baptist Church, Ann Arbor, Michigan

Former President, Phi Beta Sigma Fraternity

Keynote and Motivational Speaker

State of Alabama "Governor Appointment," Athletic Commission (three-year term), 1987-1990

Member of Big Brother Association

University of Michigan Football (three-year letter winner)

Youth Counselor, St. John's Baptist Church, Tacoma, Washington

Board Member, Mobile Sports Hall of Fame, 1995

Youth Leader, First Nazarene Baptist Church, Camden, New Jersey

Outstanding Young Men of America, 1978, 1983, 1984, 1988 and 1992

International Who's Who of Professionals, 1997, 2002 and 2006

Recipient of Associate Membership for
Mobile Sports Hall of Fame Award

Human Visionary Award, Black Who's
Who, Columbus, Ohio, 2004

Former Member, Seattle Seahawks, NFL

Lifetime Member of the Michigan Alumni
Association and the "M" Go Blue Club

Minority Opportunity Award from the University of Michigan

President and Founder, "AOK" (Athletes, Opportunities, and
Kids) Enlightening Youth Foundation in Columbus, Ohio

Stay focused and let any bit of discouragement be a momentary lapse. You cannot sell yourself as the *it* candidate if you don't believe you *are* the *it* candidate.

Networking: More Than Just Asking for a Job

Networking is about building social and business contacts. When meeting with top executives or people who are above you in the professional world, your first instinct may be to ask for a job—this is not how you network.

When you network, you want to connect with as many people as you possibly can. In fact, the person you talk with may be able to give you a job, but they can also connect you with someone who could give you a better job or better advice. Try asking the person you talk with the names of two or three people in their network—build leads and a base of names and references. This will put you further ahead in the long run.

Attending community events and other public meetings or dinners is a great way to network. When you add people into your network, let them know that you are just as willing to connect them with others in your network. Doing this will allow the two networks to merge, and both parties automatically double their network. Collect business cards and build a database to reference. Additionally, there are networking groups such as www.LinkedIn.com and www.ExecuNet.com.

Networking should be a subconscious daily act. As a part of your strategy to achieve what you want to be and where you want to be, you should make networking a top priority. Sometimes, choosing the number one pick will come down to who they know, not what they know. If the person making the final decision has two top candidates, with equal skill levels, and they personally know or know of one of your references, then *you* will be the top pick.

Dos and Don'ts

Check This List Twice When Prepping for the Process

As was mentioned earlier, making a good first impression is important and is the first step to being the number one unique candidate. Your resume is your very first impression and could be the only chance you get to make an impression. Make your resume stand out in a positive way; professionalism is key. If your skills do not lie in design and word-smithing of documents, you should consider having a professional lay out and polish your resume before you send it out to potential employers. The presentation of your resume could be the thin line that determines if you get a first interview or not. Also, remember to bring an extra copy of your resume with you to the interview.

Once your resume gets you in the door and you have an interview scheduled, you want to be sure you don't skip over minor details. Know where the interview site is located. If time allows, do a test run so that you will know exactly how long it will take you to get from Point A to Point B. Arriving fifteen minutes early for your interview is expected; being on time is considered being late. Promptness, showing your eagerness to begin the interview, is one aspect that plays into making you the number one pick.

Knowing what to expect at the interview and how they will conduct the interview will put you at ease and give you the advantage over other competitors. Do research to find out what type of interview they will put you through—a traditional interview with broad questions or a skills-based interview where you will be asked to perform simulated tasks. Spend time prior to the interview thinking about the questions you will be asked and how you will answer them. Don't memorize your answers, but be prepared with topics or key points you want to hit on while answering questions. Not only should you be prepared to answer questions, but you should be ready to ask them as well.

Many interviewers will turn the interview around on you and have you ask them questions. Be prepared by knowing background information about the company so you can ask educated questions about the company and your desired position. Part of doing your research before an interview is knowing who will be conducting the interview. If the person you are supposed to meet with has an unusual name, take all steps possible to learn and memorize the proper pronunciation of their name. It is just another small detail that could set you up as the number one pick.

Go into an interview presenting yourself in a professional manner. Treat the receptionist or administrative assistant with respect. You never know how much influence this person holds on your potential future boss. Regardless of how you are treated, when you are in the building or even close to the building where your interview is being held, never disrespect anyone. The person who will interview you could be watching, and showing poor character will not put you as their number one pick.

Before going into an interview, refrain from popping in a piece of chewing gum or smoking a cigarette to calm your nerves. Chewing gum while talking and being interviewed will not impress the interviewer. Also, some people are allergic to smoke; entering an office with the smell of smoke on you can be considered offensive and disrespectful. Cell phones and PDAs are disrespectful as well—turn yours off, or leave it in the car. It is unacceptable to answer your phone during an interview. Well-groomed men remove earrings and facial jewelry, make sure shoes are polished or clean, and wear a dark or charcoal gray suit with a light-colored shirt and power tie (red or bright color).

Even if you have been living on rice and canned meat for two months, you should never act desperate in an interview. You want to convey your positive assets, but not in a way that makes them think you will take the job no matter what. This will deplete your bargaining power if you are offered the job.

Avoid bringing up any negative points about previous jobs or employers you have worked for—they could be friends or connected through a network of people you don't know about. Be honest in your answers—the truth will come out eventually.

In order to be one of the top picks, who will get a spot in their own conference room on draft day, you have to take the necessary steps to be the ultimate number one pick. Follow your strategy through until the end, and don't leave out the small details; they are sometimes the most vital points in the process. Have the mindset of a number one draft pick, and you can be what you want to be and go where you want to go.

CHAPTER 6
Preparation: Ready, Set, Go

"Before everything else, getting ready is the secret to success."
Henry Ford

Do you remember racing or playing hide and seek as a child? Someone would count to three if you were racing and then holler, "Ready, set, go," and you would take off in an effort to win the race. If you were playing hide and seek, the person would say, "Ready, set, go," and you would have to find a hiding place. Life has changed from those days. Preparation for life and a job takes a little more than a count to three.

READY—Who Do You Know and Who Knows You?

Networks are people talking to each other, sharing ideas, information, and resources. Networking is a verb—something that you have to act on, continuously work to make beneficial. Networking goes both ways, you give away information to others, and they give you information.

1. First, identify contacts and organizations you want to network with. Subscribe to trade publication and business journals to get additional information. Become a member of key organizations that are appropriate for your field or scope of responsibility. In addition to outside resources, determine key resources within your organization that will

support your programs and initiatives or provide valuable information. Make sure those people you have identified as people you want to network with excite you, inspire you, challenge you and make you grow.

2. Second, make contact with key people and organizations. It's who you meet that counts. It's important that you identify those people and organizations who will build on your skill sets, enhance your experience and knowledge, and provide resources.

   Within your organization, make sure, if you are new, to have touch-base sessions with key leadership in all areas of the business. Even if you don't work with them directly after your touch-base meeting; it's always beneficial to know who the decision makers and supporters are. If you have been in the organization a long time, make sure you touch base with new leaders as they join the company for the same reason.

   As a member of some professional organizations, attend their major annual conferences. Get on their mailing list for their newsletters. Ask to put articles in these publications from your expertise. This gets your name out in front of others and also promotes your company's practices at the same time.

   Make sure you are meeting the key decision makers in the organization. Getting to know the person who makes decisions is the key to your success. Collect and keep business cards for a reference. Call people and companies that you know for a referral if you can't identify the right person within a company to go to.

3. Third, build relationships. Effective networkers understand that word of mouth is a way of life and building an effective

word-of-mouth network requires cultivating relationships. These relationships require time, energy, persistence, and patience. Building on common interests is always a way to develop relationships with people. Share information among each other that will benefit both parties. If offered to speak at seminars or conventions, do it. It is a great way for you to meet people.

4. Fourth, differentiate yourself from others. Use key words. Have a platform for those initiatives you are passionate about and have pioneered. Eventually, people will associate you as the expert for a certain topic and they will utilize you as their resource. You should do the same with others.

SET— Making Connections That Count! Are Your Business Cards and Calls Compelling?

How many business cards have you collected in your life...100, 200 or 300? It seems like everyone is handing out business cards. That's not a bad thing, but you need to make your card pop and stand out from the crowd. I think that there are some guidelines that you can use to make yours stand out from the regular, run-of-the-mill cards.

1. Determine your intentions. That is, what message do you want people to receive when they look at your card? Should your name or credentials stand out, or is the service you offer the primary focus?

2. Determine the format that you want to use with your business cards. Look for a text font and size that will jump out at people. Always keep in mind that the ability to read the words is more important than their impressive nature. Think of other graphics you might want on the card, such as a company logo, pictures that depict your

field of expertise, or possibly a nice border, but don't overdo it either.

3. Business cards should be kept current with the most updated information regarding how to contact you—phone number, direct extension if possible, fax number, email address, and mailing address.

4. Make sure you have the name and title, if possible, of the decision-maker you desire to reach. Have the direct office phone number versus the main office phone number.

5. Provide a warm greeting to the person who first takes your call.

6. Identify yourself, ask to speak to the decision-maker, and describe the nature of your call.

7. Once you reach the decision-maker, re-introduce yourself. Ask if they have a few minutes to speak with you or if there is another preferable time. If okay, proceed with explaining why you are calling. This is a time to reinforce your knowledge of their background, company, and expertise. Note specific instances regarding them or their company that may ignite the conversation, such as a time you have met previously or a key article.

8. Establish rapport and common interests.

9. Determine if key information could be shared at this time. Determine the preferred communication vehicle.

10. Follow up on the conversation with an e-mail or personal note thanking them for their time and indicate that you look forward to their working relationship going forward.

I always tell people to read the shareholders' filing and annual report, read the executive reports background, and go to the company's website. Know as much information about that company as possible. Pull news articles and make yourself a booklet about all the information that you gather about the company. Be ahead of the game. Get out in front and do your work. Be on your toes. Find out who knows someone in the organization. Find out the information that will help you get your foot in the door.

GO!

Now that you have the interview, it's time to get your thinking cap on. One of the most common interview questions asked is, "Tell me about yourself." Plan ahead of time how you are going to answer this question. You want to take full advantage of the opportunity by pointing out your strengths during these few minutes. This is your time to sway the employer's mind in your direction. Give them a brief overview of your most recent experience that is relevant to the position you are applying for. It is best to start with your most recent job and work your way backwards. Then move into your more personal qualities about yourself, such as being very organized or result-oriented, and other things that you want them to know. After you have finished talking about yourself, move into asking the employer a question so that you can find out exactly who and what they are looking for in an employee. By all means, don't go on and on, but try to keep your response to within two minutes.

Speak clearly and in a pleasant tone of voice during the interview. You don't want to be too loud or too soft so that they can't hear you. Smile as you have the opportunity to do so.

If asked what your weaknesses are, be smart but honest in how you answer. You don't want to say that your weakness is that you hate to work, because you have just talked yourself out of the job. However, if one of your weaknesses is that you hate to answer the telephone, you need to come up with a creative way of saying that, such as, “I get so focused on my work that a telephone that constantly rings is a distraction and does not allow me to do my best work.”

The day has come, and you are in the negotiating phase of getting the job. You are called in for a second interview. You are excited about the job, but the salary quote came in a little lower than what you expected. The last thing you want to do is take yourself out of the job right after you get it.

In order to negotiate a better salary, first, do some research and learn as much as possible about this company that wants to hire you. Find out what the average pay is in the industry. Know going towards what your bottom-line acceptance is. There are always factors such as unions that can prevent the employer from paying you more. The final decision will be yours if you want the position or not.

If you are a person in a high-demand position and other companies are considering hiring you, then you can use that as leverage to get more money. Don’t act cocky or like you are the best thing since sliced bread; humbling yourself will gain you more respect.

Let the employer mention the salary to you and don’t you ask about it in the interview. Make yourself clear when the salary is mentioned and let them know if you are willing to negotiate.

It is so important that the employer knows the benefit of your skills. Let them know how you can benefit the company through saving them cost, increasing productivity, and anything else that you can bring to the company—make them see you as their future number one asset in the department you are applying for.

Keep a straight face if they offer you a really low salary. Simply nod your head, and that little gesture might cause the employer to offer you more money. Be reasonable in what you want based on what the position is worth. Also, it is very important to be flexible in what you desire salary-wise. You know what you can and cannot live on.

Believe in who you are and what you have to offer. If you can show them all that you have to offer and handle it just the right way, you could land the job of your dreams with a salary higher than you thought.

CHAPTER 7

Interviewing: The Two-Minute Warning

Before putting his foot on the ground of the parking lot in front of the downtown high rise, he straightens his tie, checks his teeth to make sure he is free of all crumbs from his breakfast bar, and runs his hand over both shoes as a last-minute, makeshift shoe shine. His mind races as the elevator clicks with each passing floor as it moves closer to his seventeenth-floor destination, where he will be drilled and picked apart at his third interview this week. His fingers are shaking as he reaches toward the office door; he knows that, like the other two companies, this one will ask just as many in-depth and mind-boggling questions. Like the early morning dewdrops on the grass, his sweaty palms leave drops of sweat beading off the doorknob as he opens the door and walks in. Greeted by a kind smile, he momentarily focuses and explains he is there to see Mr. Jones. The pressure is overwhelming, and he faints before he can finish telling the woman with the kind smile who he is there to see. Does reading this scenario ring a bell of familiarity in your mind? Maybe it was just a nightmare you had the night before an interview, or it could be a reality for you, and that's why you're reading this book. Understanding and practicing the proper techniques for interviewing will put your mind to rest and allow you to dazzle everyone who interviews you.

Knowing what to expect in an interview and what the interviewer expects from you is the key to walking out of an interview as a success and promising option for the available position. However, there are two types of interviews you need to be aware of and be capable of participating in. There is an informative interview and an actual job interview. Both interviews have their own agenda. Preparing and understanding the concept and sometimes unspoken guidelines of each one will empower you as you work to accelerate your career.

Understanding

Before tackling the details of two types of interviews, you must first understand basic principles of human nature and how to apply them. Know that people like to say *Yes!* Think about it like this. When you have a list of phone calls to return, which ones are you more likely to make top priority: the ones where you are saying *yes* to whatever it is they are asking or the ones where you are saying *no?* To be put in a position of delivering negative news or rejecting someone, something, or an idea is not a pleasant feeling. Admit, you like to feel good, and in the same respect, the person you interview with is human and likes to say *yes* as well. Remember that people like and need honest recognition. This plays into the notion that basic human nature is to seek out the good feeling. A prime way to give people recognition is to ask their advice. By asking for advice, it shows that you respect them and value their opinion. Finally, the majority of people do not like to be put under pressure. Take a gradual approach when pursuing anything you want in life. By avoiding tense pressure and decision-filled moments, you will be more likely to get the results you are looking for.

The Informative Interview

Keeping the basic concepts of human nature ingrained in your mind is imperative when you are participating in any interview, especially an informative interview. In the informative interview, you are not interviewing for a specific job. It is merely a discussion with someone who, once they get to know you through the interview, will remember you when they become aware of an open position you are perfect for. You are there to gather information and make contacts. Never ask for a job when you are in an informative interview; it would be far too presumptuous to assume they have an open position or know of one at the current time. But this does not mean you cannot openly talk about the fact that you are actively looking for a position. By asking for a job, you would be putting pressure on them and going against the basic ideas of human nature.

Here is an explanation of the five simple purposes of an informative interview. Your first goal is to establish rapport with the person you meet with. To do this, you want to work to find out who they are, and help them to understand who you are and what your mission is. Show a genuine interest in everything they have to say; they will be able to tell if you are really interested. This is where they will learn your attitude and true character. Portraying a genuine interest in others is not a practiced or learned habit. If you have difficulty with this, you should revisit who you are and what you stand for so that you can appreciate the qualities, thoughts, ideas, and hobbies of others.

The second purpose is the exchange of information. You are there to learn from them and possibly receive other contacts from them. However, as it is with networking, you must be prepared to give as well. It is a time to gather information about your specific job market. Knowledge is power, and the more you have, the further ahead you will be. You are looking for information about the latest developments, which companies are doing what, additional articles or publications you may not have access to, trends in the market, and professional associations relative to your field of work. Before entering the interview, set the goal to leave with more information than you walked in with.

In the interview, you will give the interviewer your personal market campaign for the purpose of getting advice and a reaction to your professional brand. You want to get their comments and feedback on your performance and overall presentation. Sincerely asking for their advice may show them that you consider them an expert in their field. This will please and fulfill yet another aspect of basic human nature.

Meeting with someone for an informative interview adds them to your personal network, and should allow you to walk away with another referral. By taking the time to help them understand who you are, your vision, goals, and future aspirations, you will make them feel as though they have invested in your life. If you have successfully portrayed your message, they will feel as though they are a part of your dream and will want to contribute to it. The only exception for getting a referral for another informative interview is if that person is interested in putting your talents to work for their company or organization.

The informative interview does not end when you walk through their office door as you leave. Instead, you want to ask their permission to keep them informed on your progress. Keeping them informed about your professional advances makes them feel good and as though they are contributing to your life, and yet again staking claim on the basic ideas of human nature.

Informative Interview—Type II

The type II informative interview is much like the one mentioned above, but there are steps you must take prior to going into the interview, steps that will get you the interview. The idea of the referral interview is to establish a solid rapport with the interviewer and to create an environment for purposeful discussion for your career. You will look to gather useful information about and advice that is relevant to your career. In the referral interview, you should have a business demeanor that is matched with a cordial smile and personality; it will put both yourself and the interviewer at ease during the meeting.

The first step is to write a letter of approach. In this letter, your goal is to introduce yourself and your wish to learn from them. When writing the letter, it is important that the tone of the letter is written in a way that parallels your personality. Remember, you are not asking for a job, simply a meeting to introduce yourself and your career path. You can mention something along the lines that you are currently researching alternatives for your future career path that will utilize your leadership and keen management skills. If you have someone in your network who suggested you interview with that person, tell the interviewer that person spoke very highly of them and their knowledge in the field, and that is why you are interested in meeting with them.

To follow up with your initial letter of approach, you will need to make a telephone call to set up an appointment. Whether talking to the administrative assistant, receptionist, or the actual person you wish to meet with, you want to be sure to reiterate your purpose and intentions for the meeting. It will be more difficult to set up a meeting or interview if you do not specifically say that you don't expect them to know of any openings or to offer you one.

Preparing for the actual interview is the next step and most crucial. You are the one who has requested the interview, so it is your responsibility to make the most of that person's time. Know your specific objective, the information you hope to gain during the referral interview, and what you hope to accomplish. Some example questions are:

- What growth opportunities do you see in my career field?

- How do you see the economy affecting my business in this area within the next few years?
- Do you see your industry facing any problems in which I would be able to contribute my skills as a solution?
- What income level should I expect to reach with my background and qualifications?
- What steps do you think I should take to improve my marketability to companies?

Always check to make sure the interviewer has a vivid understanding of where you have been and where you hope to go in your career. Once you know they have clear understanding of you and your purpose, you can continue to ask questions. If they are doing the majority of the talking, then you should feel a sense of accomplishment within as you take notes, knowing that you have succeeded in the referral interview. Before leaving the interview, you will want to ask for a referral to others who could aid in accelerating your career. An example would be if you're in the insurance business, ask the person you are interviewing with if they have any contacts in commercial industries who might be interested in what you have to offer. When asking for a referral, don't expect them to give you one right away. Tell them you will check back in a few days to see if they have thought of someone in their network and from whom you could both benefit. One strong referral will get you much further than several weak ones. As with any interview, you want to always express your gratitude to the person you met with.

Within forty-eight hours, you should have a thank-you note in the mail to them. It is one component to personal marketing strategies that many overlook. Effective thank-you notes are legible, handwritten, brief, enthusiastic, positive, sincere, and unlike your resume and cover letter (*Exhibits 4A and 4B*). Open your thank you letter with the traditional (*Exhibit 5)* "Dear (first name)" or "Dear Mr./Mrs. (last name)." Choosing which one you use will depend on the nature of the relationship you have established with the recipient.

In the first paragraph, you should acknowledge your gratitude, define the benefit to both parties, and show your interest. Paragraph two is the extra mile. Choose only one of these three points for paragraph two:

Introduce one added value—use a personal success story based on topics discussed during the interview or meeting.

Clarification—used to strengthen any incomplete or unsatisfactory response you may have given during the interview.

Follow up—used to provide any additional information you did not say in the interview.

Take a more personal and fresh approach to closing the letter:

Yours with all my appreciation,

Yours in appreciation,

With all gratitude,

Finally, sign your first name below the closing and print your first and last name under your signature. It is also important to have your complete name, address, telephone number, and current date on the letter.

The Job Interview

In any interview, knowledge is power. This does not include the knowledge you need to do the job you are applying for, but rather the knowledge you retain about the company you are interviewing with. Researching the company has numerous benefits. Reading information from the chamber of commerce, trade journals, stock reports, news articles, and annual reports will give you the background information you need to ask the interviewer educated questions about the company. It will also allow you to know if you are a right fit for the company.

Going into the interview, you must remember that you are not the only one in the room looking for a solution to your problem. You are applying for a job because the company finds it necessary to hire someone to fill a position that will solve a problem within their company. Do not be so self-consumed with your need for a job that you go without understanding why they need you for the job. You want to be clear on the responsibilities for the position, how the interviewer expects the position to contribute to plans for growth and expansion within the company, and specific problems the position will address. The strongest presentation of your skills will be made when you make it applicable to their company and present yourself as their solution. Actively listening and pinpointing the company's needs will show that you are interested and will lead to a second interview.

No Pressure—Stay Positive

One question you need to be prepared for is the infamous "Tell me about yourself" question. This is what I call the Two-Minute Warning because if it takes you longer than two minutes to answer, then you have lost the attention of the interviewer. Be prepared to highlight your strongest experiences in previous jobs that will clue the interviewer in to your effectiveness to do the job.

Give brief examples that are listed on your resume. You can keep their interest by highlighting your entire work history in terms of accomplishments, results, and success. The Two-Minute Warning, "Tell me about yourself" section is absolutely the most vital part of the interview. Human nature, instinct, and emotions do play a factor in the interviewer's decision to offer you a position. The Two-Minute Warning monologue of sorts gives them a sense of your compatibility and competence to fill the position. Keeping a balanced chemistry within their company is very important; that is why the interviewers' gut feeling as to how they *feel* about you will play a role in their decision-making process. Giving their "gut" a positive response to chew on will make them feel like they are taking less of a risk by possibly hiring you.

Their Problems Are Not Yours to Solve, *Yet!*

Because all parties in the interview have an objective and problem to solve, don't be overly confident in solving the problems of the interviewer. To test your knowledge and competence, they could ask your advice on a current situation within the company. Bite your tongue and impulse to tell them what to do; you don't want to make the mistake of offending them. Instead, suggest that you have the skills to solve it, but because you are not familiar with the culture and procedures within the company, you would feel it would be unfair to make such strong suggestions. To reassure them of your skills, you can briefly recall a similar experience you have encountered and how you worked to find the best solution.

The Second Stage of the Job Interview— Power Shifts

After one or more grueling yet successful interviews, you are offered the position. The minute they offer you the job, the tables turn, and the power to negotiate lies in your hands, but before that moment, you should not discuss the topic of potential salary.

Key factors are your confidence in your own personal assets and an understanding of the prospective employer's problems and goals. Finding and effectively communicating a strong correlation between these two factors will add value to you.

When you are shopping for anything of value, you want to get the most for your money, right? Well, so does your future employer, and you are the something of value they are shopping for. Their goal is to buy you for the lowest reasonable price. But you are responsible for showing them you have value, and placing the highest reasonable price on your services is your top priority. The future employer already knows the salary limits they have to offer you, but they could strategically ask you what you think you are worth. This is like a trick question from your fifth-grade math exam. Don't answer with a specific number; instead, tell them that you don't want to be presumptuous in assuming what the job is worth, and ask what figure they have in mind. If they want to know your salary history, tell them that your previous salaries were based on different skills and services and it would be misleading to quote past salaries. They could also ask you what you need to live on, which could be an easy question for you to answer, but like the other salary-related questions, don't answer it. Remember, you want to get paid according to *worth,* not your *needs!* Respond by telling them that money isn't on the top of your agenda, but you do have a lot to offer their organization. Also, tell them that you want your salary to be based on your value to them. If they do offer an exact figure, and you don't know how to respond, stay silent. This tells them that you are considering the offer and you are not fully satisfied with it either. Silence will not do anything but remind them that they made a commitment to you and that they are buying you for a position. If you do not say anything, they could instantly offer up a higher number; they have room to negotiate, but will also have to first consider what is best for the company.

Accepting a salary offer should only happen under the *right circumstances* and at the *right price*. Achieve this goal by ensuring your skills are being used in the best possible way and in an environment that will allow you to grow and produce results, and the right price is the highest that the employer is willing to offer. Once you have received the highest possible offer and discussed benefits, take at least twenty-four hours to consider the offer and make your decision. This is customary practice, and by no means will they turn around and offer the job to another applicant while you consider what should be their very generous offer.

CHAPTER 8

Being a Sponge: Absorbing and Learning

"Live as if you were to die tomorrow.
Learn as if you were to live forever."—Ghandi

Diplomas, certifications, and various trophies exemplifying your prestigious achievements grace the walls of your office, and with each achievement you worked toward, you studied, researched, or completed hands-on training. With each achievement, you have the satisfaction of seeing your life or career progress into another, more advanced stage. No accomplishment is attained without putting forth effort; each requires you to follow a specific plan for learning. To reach a higher level, either in life or in your career, you must never close the door to learning.

Learning does not necessarily mean you have to sit through classes and workshops; rather, it should take place on a daily basis. It is a way for you to keep your mind sharp and expand your knowledge. There are verbal and non-verbal forms of learning, and because new technology and methods are produced every day, you must seek out daily learning opportunities. Reading magazines, online journals, and news articles, participating in online forums or being an active member of business or academic groups will put you in the position to grow your knowledge. Read everything you can, and continue to stimulate your mind so that you can stay current, which will lead to success.

Think about the past five years and how online networking sites (e.g., LinkedIn and Plaxo) have grown to dominate the web and the minds of so many—the dot-com world in general changes so drastically in such short periods of time that if you don't keep up to date, you will be left behind. In the past, when you searched through job descriptions, you were considered a top candidate if you had a bachelor's degree. Now, with the number of college graduates expanding, some positions that used to accept a bachelor's degree as acceptable knowledge will not look at your resume unless you have a master's degree. This is because businesses know top candidates never stop learning. By having two degrees, you are telling them that your learning experience is never-ending.

The government has recognized the importance of quality continuous learning when the No Child Left Behind program was enacted in 2001 and implemented in public schools. It is designed to make sure that children who may be disadvantaged get the best education and chance for learning and comprehending information that is possible. The goal is to close the gap between those who are advantaged and those who have complications with learning under normal circumstances. No Child Left Behind has developed special tutoring and after-school assistance for children who need additional help outside the classroom. This program is acknowledging that quality education and constant learning are important in all stages of life.

Lou Holtz is the only coach in the National Collegiate Athletic Association's history to lead six different programs to bowl games. Additionally, he is the only coach to have four different programs in the final top twenty rankings. You might say he believes that it is each individual's personal responsibility to be excellent and to continue learning.

Goals

"Life takes on meaning when you become motivated,
set goals, and charge after them in an unstoppable manner."
Les Brown

Everyone has an idea of what goals are, but ultimately, it is an objective you set and create purpose to achieve that goal. Without goals, you have no purpose. You need to set both short- and long-term goals to work towards so that you can create purpose in everything you do. If there are areas in your life where you are unable to set goals, then they have no purpose and you are wasting your time on trivial things that do not propel you forward in your life and career.

Explore the areas in your life where you desire to grow and set goals. Write them down, and remember, you have to be SMART to reach your goals—Specific, Measurable, Attainable, Realistic, and Time-bound.

Specific—You cannot reach goals if they are not clearly defined. Avoid using vague terms or phrases like *rich, successful, healthier,* or *ahead of everyone else.* Instead, state exactly what it is you want. It should be precise enough that you are able to create a vision in your head of what life will be like when you reach it. If you are setting career goals, name the specific job position you want to be promoted to, the percentage you want your income to increase by, or the project you want to be given.

Measurable—Set goals that allow you to measure your progress. The ability to track your progress will keep your focus on your goal and give you motivation to see it through until the end. Keep a record of each step you take in reaching your goal, and in times of discouragement, you can look back and see where progress has been made.

Attainable—Goals should be set according to your credentials and ability to achieve them. When you succeed in meeting your goal, you have an instant boost in confidence, and with each goal you reach, your confidence and self-esteem build. The more confidence you have in yourself and your personal abilities, the more likely you are to believe in yourself and work towards higher goals. By setting attainable goals, you are avoiding a path of self-destruction.

Realistic—If you do not set realistic goals, then you are caught in a dream world. Remember that facing your reality and being honest with yourself is the only way to set goals that are realistic in your life.

Time-bound—Once you mold your goals to fit the above specifications, you have to decide on a reasonable timeline for reaching the goals. If you do not designate a specific date or time in your life when you want to accomplish the goals, then you will procrastinate and cheat yourself out of valuable time you could have used to achieve a higher set of goals.

Commit yourself to excellence, and don't settle for less. A pastor I know put the aspect of settling for things in life into perspective. He said one of our problems is that we settle, but God does not want us to settle because He has more in store for our life than we know. When you settle, you give up. Instead, hold strong and take pride as you glow in your own self-satisfaction of attaining your goals.

Focus

"Success is focusing the full power of all you are on what you have a burning desire to achieve." Wilford Peterson

What were your New Year's resolutions? Don't remember? Or do you avoid remembering them so that you will not be reminded of your inability to reach them? Every year, new resolutions are made, but very few are ever reached. They seem simple enough, but lack of focus and vision to achieve goals is the barrier in your path to accomplishment.

Know your goals and create a focused mindset with a clear vision of the goals you plan to achieve. Developing goals without a clear focus turns the goals into an illusion, dream, or wish—all of which are solely in your imagination. Instead, you want them to become your reality. You can share your goals with a close friend or mentor and form an accountability system to keep you on track, or cut out pictures portraying your goal or the end result you are aiming for, and put them where you will see them daily.

Commitment

"Unless commitment is made, there are only promises and hopes; but no plans." Peter F. Drucker

Putting goals in place is a way to advance your life, but if you do not follow through on those goals, you need to re-evaluate your commitment level. You do not set goals you don't want to see happen. Use your strong ability to focus, and allow it to create an undeniable commitment to achieving your goals. Stay committed by tracking your progress and recognizing your hard work.

Change

"Sometimes it's the smallest decisions that can change your life forever." Keri Russell

Goals are not achieved by remaining static. You have to make changes and be open to the world of opportunities you have around you every day. Accept that life changes. Think about the way you were raised, and now, the way in which children today are raised. Neighbors do not dare discipline any children in the neighborhood except for their own; otherwise, they could face a lawsuit. Teachers do not teach the same way; now they try to teach and discipline, and discipline is not their responsibility.

Absorbing and learning does not take place using the same information because you only have to absorb and learn when things change. The world is constantly changing. Technology and its constant state of change is the basis of the fear most people have holding them back. There is the fear of feeling inadequate or ignorant performing tasks with new technology. Because technology is a part of everyday life, you have to choose whether you are going to help yourself and overcome your fear of technological changes and persevere as you work toward your goal.

When I was working for Scott Paper Company, they wanted to benchmark the best of the best. Visiting the NUMI plant in Fremont, California, revealed the high turn-over rate and poor employee morale—drastic changes were due if the company wanted to improve and surpass the competitors. Toyota acquired the company and updated it with new Japanese technology. Toyota hired the same people that made up the 75 percent turnover rate and improved the product 200 percent. Employees had to learn a new system, but the new system cultivated so much improvement that the culture of the company was reconfigured into a positive light.

W.E. Deming (1900-1993) was a world-renowned guru and author who taught into his old age. The last piece of music he composed was at age eighty-nine. He was active and continually learning, as he was regularly able to update his resume. Deming was a man who never stopped learning and absorbing, which led him to accomplish an abundance of goals in his lifetime.

The younger generations desire to be president, but have no drive to start from the bottom and work their way to the top.

Throughout their lives, the younger generations have been stroked more than others, and a sense of apathy has been imbedded in them. They want to start at the top, but they don't realize that it is all of the steps in between where they stumble that will give them the skills to be on top after they put in their hard work. There is no denying their intelligence, but that knowledge must be integrated into a team to succeed.

Change is all around, and you cannot achieve your goals until you submit to the fact that change will occur and with it, you must change your ways as well. Be a sponge. Absorb all the new information and changes so you can expand your knowledge and capacity of achieving high goals; take pride in all that you do (pride stands for Personal Responsibility In Daily Excellence).

If you want to continue to absorb and learn, make these three characteristics become part of who you are on a daily basis.

- Commit to Excellence. Make up your mind that everything that you do will be done with excellence.
- Execution. Set out to execute your goals to the fullest and be the best that you can be.
- Don't settle for just anything. Have the mindset that you will only settle for the very best.

Being a sponge and absorbing all that you can in life will set you on the right track for being the best, no matter what your goals are. Constantly positioning yourself to learn all that you can will make you invaluable to any company. Be like a sponge and continue to absorb all that you can, because learning never ends.

CHAPTER 9
The Pride of Success

"Success comes in cans, failures in can'ts." Unknown

"God gave us two ends...One to sit on and one to think with. Success depends on which one you use; heads you win—tails, you lose." Anonymous

On your way home from work, the smell of new leather is unmistakable as you are cozily driving in your luxury car. You feel a sense of satisfaction and completion in your life, and you can't help but look in the rearview mirror to see the slight grin on your face and think about all the things you have waiting at home for you—the long driveway leading up to an extraordinary house that just so happens to be your dream house, the four-car garage that houses fancy cars. Above the garage is your twenty-seat, full-blown movie theatre, and from there, you have hand-picked every detail within the property, even down to the Olympic-size pool and custom landscaping in the backyard.

This could be you, or it could be someone you envy. You look at their life and see "SUCCESS" as the headline of their life story. But examine a little closer, and reality is not as sweet as the Godiva chocolates sitting in the crystal bowl on the custom coffee table. Some see success as defined by financial and materialistic status. But that's not true success. My definition of success varies from that of most. I see success as having the total package—physically, mentally, emotionally, and spiritually.

The Journey to Success

Society has mangled the meaning and misconstrued the view of success to the point where you have to dig deep and know who you are and what you stand for before you can develop your definition of success. It is a subjective term which takes on various meanings to different people. When you are at a luncheon, cocktail party, or other social event, conversation starters consist of asking you what neighborhood you live in, what type of car you drive, where you work, or who you know. But the person who asks these questions really doesn't care about you or where you live; they are merely taking a mental inventory of what you have to see where you measure up under their definition of success that is centered on the almighty dollar.

People are constantly judging based on material things, but these trivial things in life are not what define success; rather, it is the internal satisfaction you have with your life that determines whether you are a success or failure. Others can judge all they want based on the things they see, but true success lies in what they cannot see.

When I was growing up, people would comment on how well my family had it made. The truth was, we always had what we needed, but not necessarily what we wanted. As a youth, I remember foolishly laughing at people who lived in what I called the projects, which were really just low-income housing apartments. I even pre-judged a young lady who lived there, just because she did not smell good, I would call her bad names and make fun of her. Looking back, I am ashamed at my youthful ignorance and disregard for her feelings. I also grew up with people who now work for the city's sanitation department, but just because I am an executive, it does not put me on a higher level than they are on. Their job is just as honorable and noteworthy as the work that I do. Everyone has a place in this world and plays a key role in it; remember this, because you should never judge anyone for the position they hold or job they do just because you think you are better than they are.

Shakey Jake was the town symbolic figure in Ann Arbor, Michigan, where I was attending college. He would hang out around the campus and was always dressed nice (affectionately in wild-colored clothes with his black fur coat and guitar), but for some reason lived on the streets. As would most college students, my friends and I would laugh and joke about him when we would see him. One day, I asked him why he lived on the streets, and he replied by saying that it was home for him because it was comfortable for him. Shakey Jake taught me that his measure of success was not defined by where he was, which was homeless, but what he did for others. He played music that made people happy, and for him, that was living a successful life, to bring happiness to others.

There was an article printed that said kids are smarter than adults—an interesting hypothesis, but one I thought could easily be proven wrong. However, the article addressed the satisfaction and unselfish love that four-year-olds have. They quoted young children on their definition of love. Each was innocent and enlightening because their perspective is untainted by the world's views. Imagine asking a child between the ages of four and nine years old to see what they thought success was. My thought is that their answer would be oddly shocking, but when analyzed, they would be telling the truth because their definition of success has not been changed or drilled into them by society.

Success does not have to do with self-perception, but rather your inner feeling of contentment and satisfaction. Are you able to take care of yourself and those you are responsible for providing for? If you give 100% in every task and responsibility, then you are successful.

A man who has walked the dreary road to success is Tyler Perry. Throughout childhood, he was plagued by physical abuse and raised in severe poverty. At a young age, he wrote his first play, which was reminiscent of his childhood. Perry attempted to stage the play, but it flopped, and while trying to establish himself as a playwright, he found himself homeless for awhile until his first play took off in 1998. From there, his career blossomed, and success seems to be an inevitable theme in his life, as he now does movies, sitcoms, and plays. His life has been a journey to success, and the key factor has been that he believed in himself. All it took was for one person to believe in him as much as he believed in himself before he started on his road to success.

Success is about being in the right place at the right time. Having someone to believe in you and not giving up even when you don't believe in yourself. Continue to believe and drive until the opportunity presents itself. We are impatient...we want everything now! The next generation will be worse, because they want to be president without starting at the bottom of the ladder. It will be hard to keep this group happy. Providing continuous feedback will be a challenge toward fostering their success.

Last Call

When Dr. Keith Troy, pastor of New Salem Missionary Baptist Church in Columbus, Ohio, does his benediction, it is very powerful. He says, "What are you going to do? Come on, come on—don't delay your decision today, today, today. Take control of your life today. This is your day, your hour, your moment, your choice. Don't wait another second, another minute, or another hour, because the time is not given that you will be here tomorrow.

Come on, come on—is there another today? Live and follow your dreams. Dream, dream, dream—this is your last call."

This is your last call. You have picked up this book because you wanted a change in your life. Understand who you are, where you come from, and carry out a plan to get there. Take the first step, go after your dream, and never give up! Don't allow the naysayers to cloud or discourage your dream. This could be your last call—make up your mind today, and don't look back. Be accountable to yourself, and achieve inner success by taking that leap of faith and stepping out and leaning towards success. You are faced with opportunities for success every day when you look in the mirror—*you* are *success*.

If you would like Jeff's experience as a senior executive and support in helping you grow or build your business, or for speaking engagements, please contact him at jreeves436@aol.com or visit his website JeffreyReeves43.com.

Words to Live By

from Beverly Daniel Tatum

Treat people the way you
would like to be treated.
Be kinder than necessary
whenever you can.

Look at your goals; then
look at your behavior. If you
haven't achieved your goal,
change your behavior.

Live your vision without fear.
Never settle for mediocrity
when excellence is
always possible.

TESTIMONIALS

FROM JEFF REEVES' BRANDING SESSION

Cornell Lewis
Executive Director, the Expanding Visions Foundation
Member of New Salem Missionary Baptist Church

My overall thoughts from Jeff Reeves' Branding Session is that Jeff Reeves has inspired me to accomplish greater things in my life and my non-profit organization. I have learned to re-invent myself so that I will be desirable as a candidate for other jobs.

My key takeaways were that I did not have a true understanding of what I wanted to accomplish in this life and how to get there until I attended a session with Jeff. I began a college degree based on what his session brought out in me, and I am happy to say that I have graduated. His session helped me to realize that it is possible to know what you want and who you are if you search yourself for those answers.

Jeff gave our group a chart that showed his strengths and defined him as a person. I have used this chart in my own re-making, and it has been highly successful.

As a firefighter/paramedic, we are not the type that give our loyalty to just anyone, but I can say that I would willingly give my loyalty to Jeff Reeves. I have asked him to mentor me as I walk through this journey of self-discovery. He is accessible, intelligent, and necessary to the weave of my life's fabric.

Paul White
Member of New Salem Missionary Baptist Church

My overall thoughts from the session are that I was encouraged and proud to see a black man with in-depth knowledge on the notion of branding. Jeff Reeves has studied the concept and its effects on us within our contemporary culture.

My key takeaways are that at the time, I had a twenty-four-foot box truck making deliveries for my company with no company logo or signage on it whatsoever. I realized what a huge mistake that was. People are watching me all the time. I must be consistent in my behavior, carefully choosing the things I want to be identified with and what I want to be perceived as.

I also received tools that will help you grow personally and professionally to help develop your future. Understanding of the branding tool and technique as it may relate or motivate you in your life today. I recently committed to a travel business that uses network marketing. I now understand that I am that business, and that business is me. My actions must edify the business, and the business must edify me.

APPENDIX

Exhibit 1A

BRANDING MATRIX*

	Element	Description	Jeff Reeves
1.	Vision-Brand Description	What do I want people to think? What reputation do I want my brand to develop?	Senior HR Executive that is a strategic operational thought leader
2.	Values	Core values to market and leverage	*Big picture/visionary *Charismatic/motivational *High principles and values *Innovative *Strong leadership skills *Results-oriented *Passionate *Strategic
3.	Business Priorities	Parameters for operating	*Position that has the growth opportunity *Strategic Human Resources

4	JEFF is	Approach and methods	1. Fortune 100 experienced 2. Matrix-driven 3. Catalyst for responsibility and accountability 4. Board experienced 5. Acquisition experienced 6. Well networked 7. Motivational 8. Flexible
5.	JEFF is not	Characteristics that violate basic approach and methods	*Micro-manager *Bureaucratic *Irresponsible
6.	Leverageable Uniquenesses	Unique attributes and abilities that are marketable	1. Proven measurable results with four Fortune 100 companies 2. Driven for team success versus individual success 3. Success in identifying, selecting, and building bench strength 4. Energetic work ethic to work full/long days—day after day

			5. Chief labor strategist with union and union avoidance experience (three of the four major companies) 6. Philosophy of HR being a business partner and driving ROI, integrating strategic with tactical
7.	Visual Image		*Presence—(one-on-one and groups) *Commands respect *Well-groomed *Articulate *Polished
8.	Mission Statement	What drives all decisions	Doing the right thing and facts
9.	Tagline/ Business Motto	Taglines are benefit-driven, inspirational, or descriptive	**Be a sponge…always absorb and learn.**
10.	What People are Missing	Your beliefs on what people are misunderstanding about you	*Passion for people's success
11.	Identify Your Passions	Record those things that represent the passions of Jeff	*See excellence in development of people *Assist the growth of the organization through its human capital

12.	What Is My Market?	Who are those who can and will decide to pay for your expertise?	Fortune 1000
13.	External Barriers	Real-world roadblocks	*Geographic (very limited interest in far northeast and some portions of CA) *Excessive travel schedule
14.	Other		Commitment to the stability of my family is a high priority

This document is built as a communication tool to communicate Jeff's strength prospective organizations.

*Tony Jeary High Performance Resources—The Presentation Strategy Experts—www.MrPresentation.com

Exhibit 1B

BRANDING MATRIX*

	ELEMENT	DESCRIPTION	NAME
1.	Vision-Brand Description	What do I want people to think? What reputation do I want my brand to develop?	
2.	Values	Core values to market and leverage	
3.	Business Priorities	Parameters for operating	
4.	I am	Approach and methods	
5.	I am not	Characteristics that violate basic approach and methods	
6.	Leveragable Uniquenesses	Unique attributes and abilities that are marketable	
7.	Visual Image		
8.	Mission Statement	What drives all decisions?	
9.	Tagline/Business Motto	Taglines are benefit-driven, inspirational, or descriptive	

10.	What People are Missing	Your beliefs on what people are misunderstanding about you	
11.	Identify Your Passions	Record those things that represent the passions of you	
12.	Where Is My Market?	Who are those who can and will decide to pay for your expertise?	
13.	External Barriers	Real-world roadblocks	
14.	Other		

*Tony Jeary High Performance Resources—The Presentation Strategy Experts—www.MrPresentation.com

Exhibit 2A

Questions You Can Ask an Employer

1. Is this a new position, and how did it become available?
2. What is the best job to begin in?
3. What is the range of duties and responsibilities?
4. What qualifications are needed for this kind of work?
5. What characteristics do you most like in people to fill this position?
6. Can you draw or show me an organizational chart of your company?
7. What kind of skills does someone need to be able to do this job and be successful?
8. What would an average day be like?
9. What does the work consist of?
10. What are some of the problems one might encounter as stumbling blocks to promotion?
11. What is the largest single issue facing your staff or company now?
12. What piece of advice would you give a person who is interested in pursuing this career field?

Exhibit 2B

12 Questions Most Frequently Asked in an Interview

1. What are some of your long-term and short-term goals and objectives?
2. What do you want to do with the rest of your life?
3. Why did you choose to apply for this position with our company?
4. What do you consider to be your greatest strength and your greatest weakness?
5. How would you describe yourself?
6. What do you think it will take for you to be a success with this company?
7. How do you think you can make a contribution to this company?
8. What type of career do you see for yourself in five years?
9. What skills should a successful employee possess?
10. Are you willing to spend at least six months in a trainee position?
11. How do you work when under pressure?
12. Why should I hire you?

Exhibit 2C

Unlawful Questions—
Questions You Should Not Be Asked

1. Where were you born?
2. How old are you, and what year were you born?
3. What is your race/nationality?
4. How tall are you, and how much do you weigh?
5. Do you have a disability or handicap?
6. What is your original name?
7. What is the birthplace of your parents, spouse, or other relatives?
8. What is your religion or religious affiliation?
9. Asking you to attach a photo to your resume.
10. Asking that you provide any information regarding your marital status or children.

Exhibit 3A

WELL-WRITTEN RESUME

ANNA WALTERS *
555 First Avenue
Austin, TX 55555
Home: 555-555-5555
Mobile: 555-555-5555
name@email.com

HUMAN RESOURCES / WORKERS' COMPENSATION PROFESIONAL

Efficiency and compliance focused with a blend of generalist and workers' compensation administration experience, working on both sides of the table as an employer and employee advocate. Provided human resources support to organizations with more than 700 employees and claims administration services to Fortune 500 corporations. Generated multimillion-dollar cost savings through creation of first-time self-insured programs and significantly reduced costs through decisive actions in workers' compensation administration. Deployed strong interpersonal skills while managing internal teams, cultivating relationships with business partners and government organizations, and garnering buy-in for major change management initiatives. Strong technical skills include MS office, HRMS, and WC/Safety software.

Diverse generalist experiences spans the areas of:

Policy & Program Design | Payroll & Personnel Administration | Recruitment & Selection

Training & Development | Regulatory Compliance | HRMS

Vast workers' compensation administration experience includes:

Claims Investigation & Resolution | BWC / TPA Relations | Self-Insured WC Programs

Safety Committee Development | Safety Manual Publication | TPA Selection

PROFESSIONAL EXPERIENCE

City Auction House—Austin TX 2005-Present

Assistant to HR Manager/WC Administrator/Safety & Payroll Coordinator

Perform diverse generalist functions for a 700-employee organization, partnering with the Human Resources Manager to manage policy and procedure development, recruitment and selection, personnel and compensation administration, and employee relations. Charged with the administration of all workers' compensation claims involving directing investigation, management, and resolution efforts. Manage the company's safety program, ensure compliance with OSHA regulations, and work diligently to encourage safe work practices through ongoing training and development.

Key Initiatives & Results: (1) positioned the organization to gain approval to become a Self-Insured Employer, securing projected savings of $5,000,000 over the next 5 years; (2) earned 4% rebate on workers' compensation premiums through active involvement in local safety council; (3) cultivated support of risk management and safe work practices through the development of a fist-time safety program; (4)

developed and administered a Self-Insured Workers' Compensation program and Safety Committee.

Workers' Compensation Administration	• Played a pivotal role in gathering approval to become a Self-Insured Employer, requiring collaboration with TPA and legal council to build a convincing case to present to senior leadership; developed administration process and secured BWC administrator approval. • Joined forces with the BWC, MCO, Industrial Commission, TPA, medical providers, and legal council to expedite the administration, investigation, and resolution of WC claims. • Designed and implemented a Self-Insured Workers' Compensation Program including return-to-work and transitional work programs; developed first-time tracking database. • Developed a safety program from the ground up, overcoming a longstanding indifference toward risk mitigation, including creating a safety manual, initiating a new-hire safety training, and instituting a safety incentive program to secure buy-in at all levels.

Safety Program Management	• Earned a 4% or $35,000 rebate on WC premiums through membership in the Safety Council, attend monthly meetings, and transfer knowledge on best practices to internal management and skilled trades team members.
Personnel Administration	• Processed weekly cash payroll for more than 200 employees, monitored timecards, maintained personnel files and database, and performed reporting via ABRA and TimeStar.
Training and Compliance	• Worked with auction house and auto detailing, body, and mechanic shop supervisors to identify training needs, advise on safety requirements, and ensure OSHA compliance.

NOLAN & ASSOC.—Austin TX 1982-2005

Claims Examiner / Office Manager

Charged with increasingly responsible leadership roles for this workers' compensation claims service consulting attorneys and employers on the administration of claims. Personally reviewed claims, processed BWC and IC documents, and expedited mutually agreeable outcomes. Cultivated relationships with clients and government employees to facilitate cost-effective and productive claims resolution. Managed and trained office team of up to six full-time and four independent contractors around the state. Prepared billing and payroll, processed A/P and A/R, and reconciled the general ledger.

Key Initiatives & Results: (1) partnered with owner to develop a solid organizational infrastructure to support rapid growth and support of 500+ clients; (2) served as an expert claims examiner and maintained in-depth knowledge of workers' compensation administration and regulations; (3) oversaw entire administrative team and provided ongoing training to ensure application of best practices.

Process and System Improvement	• Served as the "eyes and ears" for legal counsel, working with the BWC to identify opportunities to expedite claim resolution, ensure fair and compliant practices, and navigate a complex, paperwork-laden, and often bureaucratic system. • Cut a laborious and time-consuming billing process from eighty to only eight hours by developing an automated system to generate billing, reports, and correspondence.

Client Relations

- Improved productivity, reduced response times, and increased organizational effectiveness, paying attention to existing systems and identifying streamlined methods.

- Orchestrated activities and workflow related to the administration of workers' compensation claims for more than 500 clients, including Fortune 500 companies such as the ABC Company.

- Maintained knowledge of state and federal regulations impacting workers' compensation administration, and trained all internal team members to ensure 100% compliance.

PROFESSIONAL DEVELOPMENT

AMERICAN SAFETY TRAINING, INC.

Essentials of Safety I—2005

14-hour OSHA approved course

BUREAU OF WORKERS' COMPENSATION

Safety and Hygiene Course—2005

Covered the fundamentals of an effective safety program and job safety and accident investigation analysis

TECHNICAL PROFICIENCIES

Human Resource Management Systems: ABRA, TimeStar

WC/Safety Management: Prognos, Safety Office Software (SOS)

Administrative Tools: Microsoft Word, Excel, and Outlook; Internet Explorer

Exhibit 3B

AMBIGUOUS RESUME

ANNA WALTERS*
555 First Avenue
Austin, TX 55555
Home: 555-555-5555
Mobile: 555-555-5555
Name@email.com

Objective: To secure employment with a progressive company in the administration of their workers' compensation program.

Experience: *2005-Present City Auction House Austin, TX*

Worker's Comp Administrator/Safety Coordinator/Payroll Coordinator

- Responsible for administration of workers' compensation claims. Investigate, manage, and resolve claims. Responsible for the development of the Self-Insured Workers' Comp program. Manage claim database, return to work, and transitional work programs.
- Work with the BWC, Industrial Commission, MCO, TPA, medical providers and legal counsel in the administration of claims. Assisted with the application and approval of right to be a Self Insured employer.
- Responsible for company safety program, investigating incidents and compliance with OSHA regulations. Developed and implemented safety training programs and

developed the company's Safety Committee. Maintain the OSHA log, generate required reports, and attend safety seminars. Enrolled in the Safety Council, earning a 4% rebate on premiums.

- Responsible for cash payroll of over 200 employees. Generate weekly paychecks; maintain personnel files and employee database.
- Assist Human Resource manager with full-time and part-time employee payroll, drug-free payroll workplace program, and miscellaneous HR functions. Responsible for daily time card maintenance and reports to all departments for accurate tracking of employee's hours.

1962-2005 Nolan and Associates Austin, TX

Office Manager and Claims Examiner

- Managed a workers' compensation claim service assisting attorneys and employers with claim processing.
- Claims Examiner responsible for claim reviews, processing BWC and IC forms, and resolving problems within claims.
- Supervised office staff, responsible for customer service, A/P, A/R, and payroll.
- Developed computer systems for billing, generating reports, and correspondence.

Education: Austin City High School / Austin, TX
Graduate 1980

- General Studies

Beauty Academy 1980-1981

- Manager's Cosmetology license obtained 1981

  Essentials of Safety 1, June 2005

- 14-hour OSHA-approved course conducted by American Safety Training, Inc.

  Bureau of Worker's Compensation Safety and Hygiene, 2005

*Source: www.dearsamonline.com

Example of a Dynamic Resume

Jeffery Jones
1211 Wilson Street
Dallas, Texas 76590
601. 456.7890

SUMMARY OF QUALIFICATIONS

Extensive experience in multi-branch operations includes the following areas:

- Successfully developing and personally marketing new products for small business.
- Rewriting and implementing branch system policies and procedures.
- Troubleshooting operations and establishing improved financial controls.
- Budget planning and controls, audits.

EXPERIENCE

Bank of the West, Dallas, Texas
1988-1999
VICE-PRESIDENT

- Assisted president and regional vice-president in charge of branches.
- Security officer, making and implementing camera placement and procedures for three branches. Wrote security manual.

- Installment loan officer, improving collections and commercial loan documentation.
- Troubleshooting assignments to Philadelphia office, establishing efficient operations and financial controls.

Sovereign Bank, Fort Worth, Texas
1970-1988
VICE-PRESIDENT

- Created new position with responsibility for commercial balances/profit and loss in a ten-branch area.
- Established program for business with under $1 million in annual sales, developing products and marketing through personal calls.
- Generated $10 million in deposits and $40 to $70 million in lending.

1965-1970
VICE-PRESIDENT- Saginaw Branch

- Managed staff of 15 employees, increasing deposits 80% to $10 million and loan totals to $4 million.

EDUCATION

University of Texas, Austin, Texas
Marketing and Business Administration (emphasis in banking)

EXTRACURRICULAR ACTIVITIES

Vice Preside of Student Assembly; President of Glee Club Tours; Member of basketball team

References available upon request

Exhibit 4A

Examples of Great Cover Letter

1211 Wilson Street
Dallas, Texas 75021
November 27, 2007

Mr. John Jones, CEO
XYZ Corporation
701 8th Avenue
Dallas, Texas 75091

Dear Mr. Jones:

My name is George Smyth, and I am interested in the Chief Financial Officer position that is available with your company. I know that this position will handle a budget of approximately $21 million dollars a year. I was made aware of your company through a private headhunter agency by the name of Executives Incorporated. I know this position is vital to your entire organization and oversees all of the budgets for the entire corporation.

I have ten years of experience doing this exact type of work. I am the CFO for the ABC Corporation with an annual budget of $18 million dollars a year. I graduated with a degree in accounting from Arizona State University and passed the CPA exam a month after graduating from college. I went on to get a master's degree in accounting from Harvard and my doctorate degree from Yale. I have attached my resume for your review. I know that I can take your organization to the next level because of my experience.

I would like to call you within the three days to schedule an interview. If you are not available within that time frame, please contact me to schedule an interview. I'm looking forward to hearing from you. Thank you so much for your time and consideration.

Sincerely,

George Smyth

Exhibit 4B

Example of Great Cover Letter

1211 Wilson Street
Dallas, Texas 75021
November 27, 2007

Mrs. Jamey Francis, Head of Clerical
XYZ Corporation
701 8th Avenue
Dallas, Texas 75091

Dear Mrs. Francis:

My name is Megan Hughes, and I very interested in the Supervisor of Clerks position. I know that your company is the number one producer of fine jewelry in the nation. I was referred to your company by the Employment Agency of Greater Dallas.

I am currently the supervisor of seven clerks with the ABC Corporation. I have been with this company for five years and have received two promotions within that time frame because of excellent job skills. As I said before, I oversee seven clerks, and each month for the past year, our department has come in first for outstanding service to our customers. Additionally, I have my bachelor's degree in business management, and I attend seminars in my major on an annual basis.

Since you have indicated in your employment ad that you would not like any phone calls, I would appreciate and look forward to hearing from you to schedule an interview within the next few days. Thank you so much for your time and attention to this matter.

Sincerely,

Megan Hughes

Exhibit 5

Example of Thank You Letter after an Interview

Mr. Richard James
VP Sales
ABC Corporation
305 Wilson Avenue, Suite 1211
Anytown, US 39648

Dear Mr. James:

Thank you for the time you spent with me discussing the Manager of Sales position at ABC Corporation.

I am very interested in the position, and I know that you will be very pleased with the quality of my work. My experience with large sale accounts, along with my attention to detail and my sharp eye for quality, will allow me to do an excellent job for you.

Thanks again for your time. I look forward to hearing from you with some good news soon.

Sincerely,
Alton David

LaVergne, TN USA
14 May 2010
182660LV00004B/1/P